HOW TO RESEARCH TRENDS

move beyond **TREND WATCHING**
to kick start **INNOVATION**

Els Dragt

COLOPHON

BIS Publishers
Postjesweg 1
1057 DT Amsterdam
The Netherlands
T(31) 020 515 02 30
bis@bispublishers.com
www.bispublishers.com

ISBN: 978 90 6369 433 3

Copyright © 2017 Els Dragt
2nd printing 2018
www.howtoresearchtrends.com
#htrtbook

Graphic design: Esther Scheide
www.vrouwtjevanpapier.nl

Made possible by: Fontys Academy for Creative Industries
www.fontysaci.nl

BISPUBLISHERS

FOREWORD | David Kester

As a design professional, I feel that the art and science of trend research is like a secret sauce. Designers often say that they are designing for our future selves. With every great breakthrough product or service, we are taking a leap into the great unknown. This cannot be done without spotting trends and identifying deep human insights.

At the end of the last century technologists at MIT forecasted the Internet of Things. By 2020 there will be over 20 billion connected devices. Today I shout at an inanimate plastic cylinder and it will play me some music or do my shopping. Leave aside whether this is a good or bad thing: what are the implications for people? And does it change my understanding, when I consider that the same algorithms can translate human voice instruction into "robotic" tasks that save lives? Voice control is now used in some hospitals for minimally invasive surgery and is proven to assist surgeons and nurses to achieve better health outcomes.

A few years ago, when I was running the UK Design Council, I commissioned a benchmarking survey across some of the world's most innovative companies including Toyota, Google and Lego. We were looking for lessons in innovation and we found rich pickings. One finding was a model for innovation that has become an industry and academic norm. Another was that a systematic approach to innovation relies on powerful research insights. Stripping aside the techniques and the jargon, it means looking at the world with a fresh approach. To change the familiar you have to see it again for the first time. This is the foundation of how we decode the world around us and become agents rather than victims of change.

I am a big fan of ethnographic and observational techniques in research. My personal conversion came during a health project for the UK's National Health Service. We were investigating new ways to combat infection. Our researchers camped out in hospitals watching, filming and observing. They came back with trends backed by very detailed insights. The outcome from this research led to a new wave of products and environments for hospitals. Without this research phase, we wouldn't have a brilliant easy-to-clean commode as a standard product in most of our hospitals.

I've been lucky enough to work with Els Dragt and hear her explain the practice and theory of research to many aspiring innovators. This book is a delight and much overdue. It demystifies one of the most important ways we turn human needs and challenges into innovation and new realities.

DAVID KESTER

David is a former CEO of the UK Design Council and founder of the Design Thinkers Academy London and the strategy studio DK&A. He is an Hon Professor at Warwick Business School and a Fellow of the Royal College of Art.

INTRO

WHY THIS BOOK?

Imagine you are at a dinner party where people ask you about your profession. You wipe your mouth, take a deep breath and tell them: "I'm a trend researcher". Then you lean back and wait for the standard response to come: "Beg your pardon, you're what?" "Well, I research trends." "Ooooh so, you're a trend-watcher! Can you tell me about the latest fashion trends and what colours to wear this summer?" Sigh!

As this conversation illustrates, the profession of a trend researcher is still highly charged with stereotypes. Many think it is mainly about hip and trendy fashion styles or about hypes and fads. I fully understand this preconception, because it was mine too. But when I started to orientate myself some more on trend research the scales fell from eyes. I was amazed about the broader scope of this profession and how it includes so much more than just hypes, styles and the latest gadgets. It studies change and provides an analysis of emerging shifts in people's needs and wants. These trend insights are essential during any innovation process as a foundation to create future proof concepts that improve people's quality of life. I would like to take trend research to a next level where organisations perceive trend analysis as an ongoing dialogue rather than just a yearly purchase of a trend report as a nice little add on. I believe it is up to trend researchers to empower organisations to produce innovative policies, strategies, concepts, products and services that in turn empower people.

To detect, understand and create change, it is crucial to develop a solid research design and execute your trend research in a structured manner. But how? When I started out with trend research I could not find many books explaining the process of trend research. There are many inspiring books and reports presenting next year's trends but they explain little about the research process behind them. There are also lots of interesting books on long-term futures studies, which have a more academic approach, but these are not so easy to use in an applied setting. Then there are insightful books written by trend agencies, showcasing their unique vision on the trend process but these are somewhat unilateral. So where is that book I was craving for as a beginner in trend research? The book that explains the process of trend research by showing multiple perspectives and brings this in an accessible and down to earth way for everyone to understand? I decided to write one myself. So here it is, in front of you.

I learned by doing, I learned by watching others, I learned by experimenting, failing and adjusting. I have worked at several agencies applying trend research for various organisations and brands, from non-profit to profit, with a local and international scope, within a variety of sectors from finance to fashion and from telecom to food. The lessons I learned during this journey I am now sharing with my students at Fontys Academy for Creative Industries (ACI) in the Netherlands. My colleagues and

I created a curriculum at bachelor level called International Lifestyle Studies (ILS) which has trend research at its heart. After years of experimenting, failing and adjusting I feel confident enough to share our perspective on how to learn the basics of trend research in a hands-on way.

FOR WHOM?

Would you like to know if this book is interesting for you? If you are looking for vague trend guru talk, then walk away from this book. If you want a demystified, down-to-earth approach to trends, look no further. This book is written for anyone interested in human-centred innovation. Whether you are a student or teacher, beginner or professional, marketer or policy maker, designer or analyst, entrepreneur or executive, researcher or strategist. Understanding trends, the emerging values and needs of groups in society, provides you with a foundation to innovate and create change.

WHAT'S INSIDE?

This book demystifies the world of trend watching and shatters the crystal ball stereotype. It gives you a candid and unbiased overview of the trend research process. It is practical, hands-on and offers multiple perspectives of professionals and (former) trend students around the globe on researching trends.
It shows you that researching trends is a skill that combines the intuitive and the analytical. It brings a structured research approach to the table. You will learn in a hands-on way to scan your environment for signs of change, analyse your trend spots and apply your trend insights to kick start innovation. The book synthesises existing theories, concepts and ideas on trend research and the interviews with experts and students will guide you on your trend journey. This will help anyone who wants to innovate and create change for the short and long term to execute their own trend research. Yes, you can do it too!

Researching trends is a journey and this book would like to be your guide. It has six chapters which allow you to time travel and immerse yourself in the process of trend research. These chapters are:

#1 REWIND - looking back at looking forward
You will start in the past, yes really! In this chapter you will become familiar with the objectives of trend research, the history of researching the future, the way past, present and future are interconnected and the status quo of the trend profession.

#2 FRAMEWORK - learning the lingo
To understand and communicate about a trend research process, you need to have a framework and know the basics about the vocabulary and theories used in trend research. In this chapter you will also be introduced to the three core phases of trend studies: scan, analyse and apply.

#3 SCAN - the art of looking sideways
The future is starting right now. How do you find manifestations of the future? In this chapter you will be updated on how to scan your surroundings for seeds of change. It includes loads of tips and tricks to conduct field and desk research in order to spot change.

#4 ANALYSE - connecting the dots
One manifestation of change is not yet a trend. In this chapter you will learn how to analyse your findings and move from trend spots to really understanding patterns of change. You will also read about the importance of naming trends and visualising them in an inspiring way.

#5 APPLY - innovate or die

How do you apply your trend insights during an innovation process? In this chapter you will define a trend scope and curate your trend research in a tailor-made way. You will complete the trend research process by translating your insights into future-proof ideas.

#6 FORWARD: the future unfolds

What does the future of researching the future hold? This chapter looks forward and showcases visions of trend professionals on moving their own profession forward. It concludes with these experts helping you move forward too by sharing their essential advice.

Each chapter includes the following elements:
» Theoretical information regarding the subject at hand, collected, analysed and synthesised from various sources in combination with experience by practice.
» Questions to activate your brain and understand the theory even better.
» Suggestions for further reading, watching and clicking. This book cannot provide a complete overview on trend research. If you are interested in a specific subject it redirects you to related sources for you to dive into.
» Interviews, quotes and tips from trend professionals and (former) trend students across the globe. These make the chapters come to life and will give an insight into multiple perspectives on each of the topics in the six chapters.

WHAT'S NOT INSIDE?

No numbers: this book does not shed light on the more quantitative approach of trend forecasting. It will not explain how to use Excel sheets and computer models to extrapolate numerical data from the past and present into the future.

No science: although I have used some academic sources in this book, it does not provide a scientific approach on exploring the future. It does not focus on the complete field of futures studies. It focuses on applied trend research that can be used in a day-to-day organisational context where deadlines and targets are a reality.

No next year's trends: this book does not double as a trend report or showcase what is hot or not. That type of information is too volatile and trends do not appear or disappear yearly on the 31st of December. It does not include many trend descriptions because I would like you to keep an open mind and not get stuck too much on one specific way of reporting trends. You can find many free trend reports online for inspiration, which I will refer to throughout the book.

HAPPY READING!

Trend research is a profession that is ever developing and this book is therefore also a work in progress, under construction and permanent in beta. You are more than welcome to contribute, add, suggest or ask anything. You can find more information and material at howtoresearchtrends.com. Okay, enough said, let's start our journey. And if we ever meet at a dinner party, I hope you will ask me all sorts of questions besides which colour you should wear this summer.

Els Dragt

TABLE OF CONTENTS

#1

REWIND

LOOKING BACK AT LOOKING FORWARD

In this chapter you will hit rewind and become familiar with the objectives of trend research and the history of researching the future. You will be brought up to date on the way past, present and future are interconnected and the status quo of the trend profession. This will help you to navigate the trend research domain and understand its roots.

‹ TOPICS

‹ INTRO

We are all futurists. We all try to think and plan ahead in some way or another. From checking the weather forecast and deciding on which activity to do in a couple of hours to thinking forward career-wise five years from now. This tendency to be curious about the future and trying to anticipate it is not a specific symptom of current modern times. For centuries there has been a constant search for ways to get a hold of uncertain futures. From the ancient Greeks visiting the oracle of Delphi to the current computer based algorithms trying to model and predict the future.

*"You shouldn't be afraid of the future but acknowledge there is
a future and try to prepare for or influence that future. Working
with trend research makes you more conscious of the future."*

Carlijn Naber - Economic Psychologist and Senior Lecturer
Trend Research at Fontys ILS

Trend research is about detecting signs of change happening right now and the directions these indicate to possible futures. In this chapter you will take a first step into the world of trend research. You will read about the reasons to research trends and how past, present and future are interconnected. You will also be updated on the history of research into the future, read about predicting versus exploring futures and last but not least pick up on the status quo of the trend profession.

WHY RESEARCH TRENDS?

Research in general is aimed at finding new knowledge. It is the systematic investigation of a certain topic in order to establish facts and reach new conclusions. But when everything in our interconnected, complex world is in a state of flux and there is a lot of uncertainty to deal with daily, is it even possible to research this? In the context of an ever changing world, trend research can be used as a method to identify and understand change in a structured way in order to be aware of possible directions of change. It can be applied to social, public and commercial challenges. Trend insights can steer one towards a more consciously chosen future and provide input to influence the future.

> *"Trend research helps to identify and capitalise on opportunities to future proof business strategies."*
>
> Sam Shaw - Head of Insight at Canvas8

A trend is a direction of change in values and needs which is driven by forces and already manifests itself in various ways within certain groups in society. Chapter two will give you more information on the definition of a trend and the framework of trend research. But why should you research trends anyway? Trend research has three main goals: detect change, understand change and act on change.

DETECT

Trend research is firstly about detecting manifestations of change happening right now. By involving yourself into trend research you will become more sensitive and open to change and you will be able to detect signs of change more easily and earlier. It helps you to develop outside-in thinking instead of inside-out. You can detect shifts in various ways, for instance by doing specific desk and field research activities, which you can read about in chapter three of this book.

> *"It is important to develop the delicate skill to spot early signals of change."*
> Laura Wolfs - Senior Research Consultant at Point Blank International

UNDERSTAND

Secondly, trend research is about understanding change. By analysing all manifestations of change and their underlying drivers you will understand these from a wider, transdisciplinary and holistic perspective. You can move beyond observations and really get a feel of what is lying beneath. Understanding change can also make you more open to change and willing to accept uncertainty. You can analyse change in various ways using clustering and validating tools, which you can read about in chapter four of this book.

> "In trend research it is important to explain the change in underlying values and needs very clearly because it forms the core of any trend analysis."
> Carlijn Naber - Economic Psychologist and Senior Lecturer Trend Research at Fontys ILS

ACT

And last but not least, trend research serves as a foundation for vision building, strategy development and guides decision making. Trend research draws your attention to likely changes and challenges. This creates a sense of urgency and influences what is on the political, organisational or your personal agenda for following years. You can act on change to improve people's quality of life (Felce, 1995) in various ways using communication and translation tools, which you can read about in chapter five of this book.

> "Trend research helps to set out guidelines for the future in an open and valid manner so we can create prosperity by increasing our quality of life and increasing profits at the same time."
> Carl Rohde - Culture Sociologist and founder of Science of the Time

FUTURES' PAST

To understand the domain of trend research you need to understand its roots. The desire to know the future emerged in many forms over the last centuries. From prophecy to philosophy to military strategy, many intellectual traditions have defined the current framework of thinking about the future and about trends. The timeline sheds some light on the genealogy of futures research and where it stands now.

TIMELINE | A HISTORY OF FUTURES STUDIES

(Son, 2015 & Asselt, 2010)

500 | RISE OF RELIGIONS

In medieval times the focus on religion played a key role in peoples' idea of the future. People's behaviour and actions during their daily life concentrated on getting to an after-life. Many religions also claim that divine prophets have the power to see into the future and change it.

3000 BC | MESOPOTAMIA

The kings in ancient Mesopotamian areas tried predicting the future using the position of stars and sheep livers. These royal men attempted to build their empires on anticipating the future of economics and politics.

1400 | RENAISSANCE

Instead of the future being determined by the stars or a divine entity, philosophers like Machiavelli argued that humans have, to a certain extent, control over their lives. In his work 'Il Principe' he states that the ability to adapt to changing circumstances is important to succeed in life. In 1516 Thomas More publishes his book 'Utopia' that initiates a tradition of utopian stories in which ideal future societies are described.

600 BC | ORACLE OF DELPHI

For hundreds of years people visited the Delphi site in Greece, relying on the oracle to help them choose the best course of action for the future. Questions varied from crop growth to love life to military strategies. The oracles given by the Delphi priestesses were rather cryptic and ambiguous. How the inquirers interpreted these divine communications shaped their future actions.

1960 | FUTURES INSTITUTES

During the sixties and seventies platforms and networks of futures studies emerged, like World Futures Studies Federation (WFSF) and the World Future Society (WFS). A period of awareness of the darker side of growing prosperity and consumerism began. In 1972 the Club of Rome published their famous report 'Limits of Growth' showing the possible future consequences of exponential economic and population growth in a world of finite natural resources.

1700 | ENLIGHTENMENT

This period shows a rise, mainly in Europe, of reason, analysis and individualism rather than following traditional lines of authority. The concept of the future becomes more open ended and the general view is that people can plan or shape the future in line with their needs to create progress in society.

1980 | GETTING WITH THE GURUS

From the nineties onwards the trend gurus entered the scene. These charismatic individuals monitored mainly short term future signals. They presented these in a visual and engaging way. They inspired many business leaders with fast paced trend talks and stimulated them to be more open to change.

1950 | PLANNING WITH MILITARY PRECISION

After the First and Second World War a period of recovery and rebuilding of nations began. Ideas about predictability and manipulability of societies became the norm. Think tanks and planning agencies popped up, like RAND, a renowned American think tank applying military techniques like scenario planning and the Delphi technique of brainstorming to think about the future.

1900 | SYSTEMATIC FUTURES THINKING

In 1902 the article 'The Discovery of the Future' by writer H.G. Wells is published in the acclaimed scientific journal Nature. Wells promotes a future forward mind-set as being more creative, masterful and modern than the predominant historical way of thinking. His views are a catalyst for the discipline of futures studies and thinking about the future in a more systematic way.

1970 | PROFITABLE FUTURES

Studies into trends and futures became more attuned to generate input for business strategies. Oil company Shell, for instance, used scenario planning techniques to prepare for possible futures like a resources crisis. When in 1973 an oil crisis became reality, Shell had already prepared for this possible future and was able to rapidly change their business strategy to become a world player in the oil industry.

2000 | THE POWER OF TRENDS

World-wide terrorism attacks and economic recessions pave the way for a more open and innovative mind-set in society: if the old ways don't work, then try new ones. Trend researchers are joining innovation teams and providing input for innovation strategies. Educational programs integrating trend research in their curriculum are on the rise.

PAST, PRESENT, FUTURE

Researching trends means that you are dealing with people's notions of the past, the present and the future. Time is a social construct; it is something we, as humans, make up ourselves. We use the past to guide our present-day behaviour, which in turn influences the way we build images of the future. How you reflect on the past and are behaving in the present influences how you perceive your future. Your thoughts on the future in turn shape your actions (Bell, 2003 & Bishop, 2012). As a trend researcher it is important to be aware of your own beliefs and perceptions of the past, present and future because this influences the way you observe the world. When researching trends it is therefore essential to understand how the past, present and future are interconnected.

PAST

You probably had to learn all kinds of historical dates and events by heart during history classes. Most of the time these lessons depict stories about the past as if they are factual information. But these historical accounts are often subjective and reflected upon from a specific cultural angle. Take, for instance, colonialism. The way history is portrayed varies strongly from colonisers' perspectives to the perspectives of the suppressed and the invaded. History is often the story people tell themselves about who they want to be. Because history is a mystery, you should not see the past as the most reliable guide into the future, although it can help to put shifts and changes into perspective. Information about the past is mainly used to understand our present day behaviour. If you would rely on the past too much you would be, as media professor Marshall McLuhan (1967) once wrote, 'driving into the future looking in a rear view mirror'.

"No single 'right' projection can be deduced from past behaviour. The better approach, I believe, is to accept uncertainty, try to understand it, and make it part of our reasoning".

P. Wack - 1985

PRESENT

Just as your reflection on the past guides your current behaviour, your behaviour in the present influences the future. Signs of change already manifest themselves right now and these can be researched. The present holds a collection of turning points which create trails into a variety of possible futures. The flipside of leaning too much on the present is that it can make you too narrow minded in seeing a variety of alternative futures. We are more open to evidence reinforcing our beliefs, than to anything contradicting them. People tend to project the present and current issues onto the future as if nothing else might change along the way: as if it is a linear, continuous storyline, while many unexpected events can change our present day reality within the blink of an eye.

"The present is no more than material for the future."
H.G. Wells - 1913

FUTURE

As the above mentioned shows, the future should not be seen as a linear continuation of the past and present. Just like time, the future is a social construct. It is shaped by people's perceptions of the past and present and by their expectations of the future. The future is in the making right now, it is being created, as we speak, by ourselves as a society. As a trend researcher you can investigate manifestations of these changes and use these as input to explore alternative futures.

"If men define situations as real, they are real in their consequences."
W.I. Thomas - 1928

QUESTION ···

Are you a past, present or future oriented person?
The way you look at the future is defined by your own time orientation.
What type of orientation do you have? Read the questions below to get
an indication which type of person you might be.*

Do you often look at your personal photographs? Are you keeping
a diary? And do you love to tell people your life story? Do vintage,
retro and dust turn you on? Then you must be the nostalgic type and
oriented towards the past.

Can you get into the flow easily while working on a project? Do you
often do something in the spur of the moment? Are you feeling totally
zen and in the now most of the time? It seems like you are a modern
day Buddha and mainly present-oriented.

Are you thinking about what might happen a lot? Do you keep an
agenda everywhere you go? Do you love horizons, horoscopes and the
next and new? You might just have a future-forward personality.

Do you feel you do not belong in any of the above categories?
Take caution: when you are neither in the past, present or future,
you might be stuck in a time warp!

*Of course this is not a certified psychological test, but you probably feel attracted
to one of these categories more than the others and this can influence how you
perceive the future yourself.

···

PREDICTION OR EXPLORATION?

A prevailing image of trend researchers is that they claim to predict the future. Statements like "In 2030 we will all have self-sustaining lifestyles, transport ourselves via self-driving cars and 3D print our food." are very common in presentations by trend gurus. On the other hand if you type in 'predictions gone wrong' in an online search engine you can find a lot of examples of experts predicting future events which never came true. Is prediction of the future possible at all? That depends mainly on how you look at the future in a philosophical kind of way. There are many different ways of looking at the future depending on your cultural background and roots. The following three approaches of the future (Asselt, 2010) are widely used:

» The future is determined. This approach sees the future as fixed and determined by fate and destiny.
» The future is open but not empty. This approach sees our future as open but not totally empty because it is partly shaped by our actions in the past and present.
» The future is open. This approach believes that the future is open and can be completely influenced by human beings.

As a researcher of trends it is important to be aware of your own beliefs and perceptions regarding the future because it will influence the way you analyse signs of change.

QUESTION ··

What are your thoughts on the future?
What are your ideas about the future? How uncertain or how determined do you feel it is? Ask yourself the following questions:

» To which degree do you think the future is determined?
Do you believe in fate and destiny?

» To which degree do you think the future is open?
Do you believe anything can happen?

» To which degree do you think the future can be shaped?
Do you believe you have the power to influence your future?

··

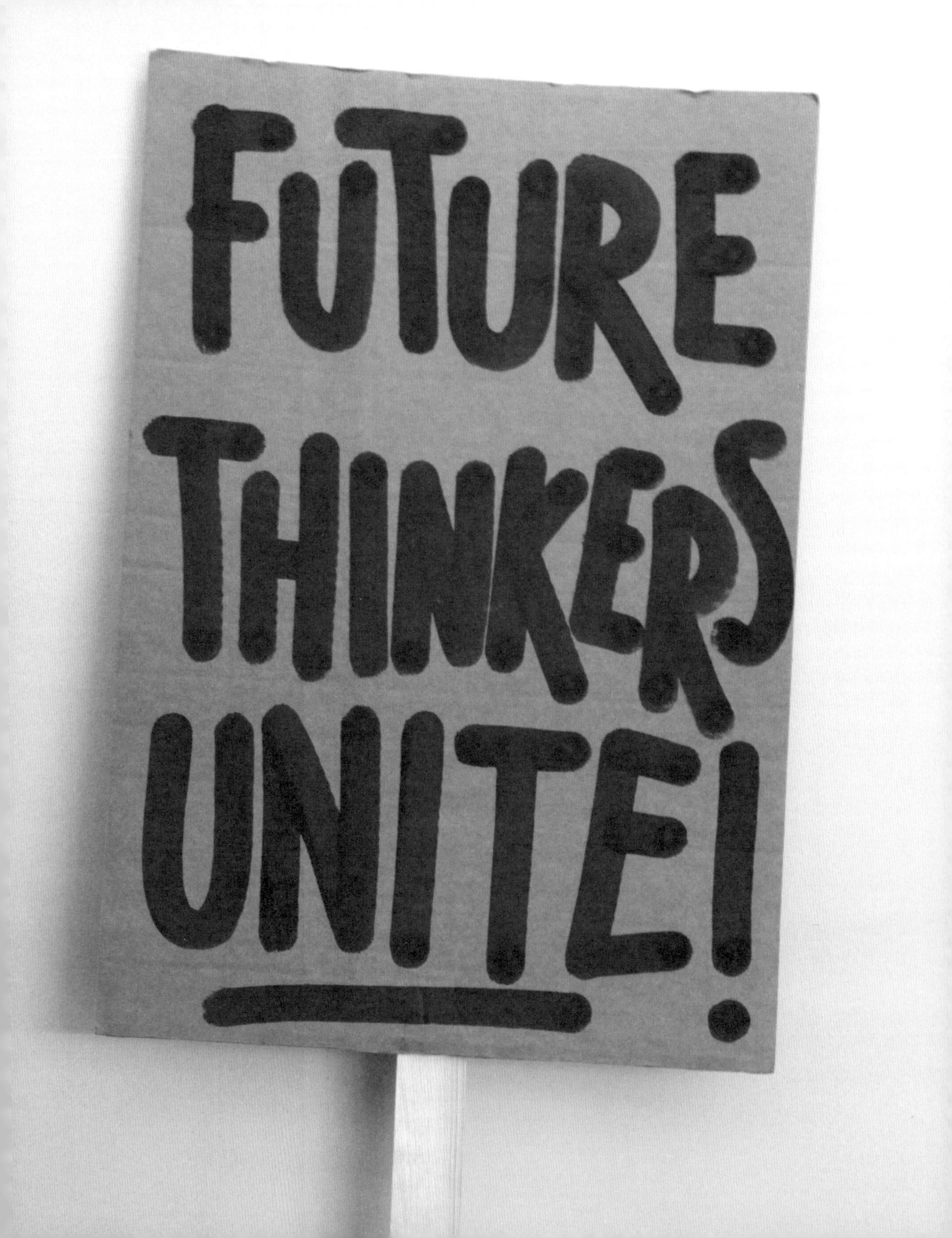
FUTURE
THINKERS
UNITE!

Many trend researchers do not see the future as an open and empty black hole but not as a fixed and upfront written storyline either. Most of them agree upon the notion that the future is uncertain and open within limits. Maybe a trend guru here or there will tell you that they can give a one hundred percent accurate forecast of the coming years. But most trend researchers take the point of view that it is impossible to accurately predict the future. There is just too much uncertainty in predicting the outcome of a process involving human beings combined with elements of nature. Next to that, information about the future cannot be verified in a classic scientific manner, because the future has not happened yet and is not seen as observable in a traditional academic way. Therefore it is not possible for anyone (yet) to predict the future with one hundred percent accuracy (Bell, 2003 & Hines, 2012).

> *"Due to unexpected events, the so-called black swans, I feel that no method or person can predict trends and the future."*
>
> Nelson Pinheiro - Assistant Professor of Trends Studies and Cultural Management at the University of Lisbon

As a trend researcher you may not be able to predict the future, but you can definitely use your trend insights to explore various futures. You can make an educated guess about how trends might play out in different ways in the nearby future. The domain of trend research provides a framework for systematic exploration of change in the future. Mind you, exploring various futures does not mean that you are merely fantasising about the future. Trend professionals will always back their trend findings with a solid analysis. And let's face it, is it not better to at least try to explore the future than to ignore it altogether?

> *"I talk about the future in ways of the past, present and the possible. There is not one singular future. I talk in plural and potential instead of singularity."*
>
> Kristina Dryža - Global Director of Trends and Futures at House of Brand Group

A PROFESSION

The domain of trend research is fairly new and some wonder if it is a legitimate profession at all. While many other professions have manifestos, codes of conduct and ethical guidelines, anyone can call themselves a trend researcher. There is not a specific stamp of approval needed from a trend inspector. The field is still very much under construction and in the midst of building a shared body of knowledge. Literature studies that try to create an overview, for example Foundations of Futures Studies by Wendell Bell, are very helpful in finding common ground. On the other hand, should a domain focused on understanding and embracing change need a rigid framework or structure at all? As Bell (2002) states, you can find examples of both good and bad work in any type of field and no field, unless it is stagnant, is free of controversy.

> *"Developing a common standard is a challenge and is it necessary? This does not really fit with the core values of the trend profession of being original and autonomous."*
>
> Tessa Cramer - Future-minded Academic and Senior Lecturer Trend Research at Fontys ILS

There is a wide diversity in backgrounds of practitioners of trend research. Every professional has their own unique trend journey. Because there was no formal education on researching trends known to them or available, many trend professionals are self-educated. Most did not even know it was a profession at all and often became acquainted with it by chance. Trend experts can have backgrounds ranging from psychology or economy to communication, design or engineering. These different backgrounds and educations make trend research a very interdisciplinary and diverse domain.

> "I have always been curious, always thinking about why people do the things they do and wanting to discover new things. I never thought I could turn that into a job."
> Erica Bol - Change Maker at Teach the Future

The variety in backgrounds also results in a wide spectrum of job titles, ranging from trendwatcher, coolhunter and forecaster to trend consultant, innovation strategist and change analyst. For the outside world this is often confusing because the differences and similarities between the different job titles are not clear. This makes it harder for people to decide who to hire or collaborate with for a trend based project.

> "Every trend researcher uses a different kind of job title and has a whole background story that comes with it. It is a job that needs an explanation, an appendix. It is very different from more clear-cut professions like a doctor or an accountant."
> Tessa Cramer - Future-minded Academic and Senior Lecturer Trend Research at Fontys ILS

Adding to the confusion is the fact that trend researchers do not have a shared consensus about definitions, terminologies and methodologies to use in trend research. Although it might not fit an open domain like trend research to have a fixed framework, the other end of the extreme of having an all-open approach overwhelms outsiders craving for some guidance. Chapter two will therefore provide a framework to use as a foundation to build your trend research on.

> "Trend researchers should use a common language or at least some kind of language that illustrates what the input and output is of their process."
> Jakob Sutmuller - Senior Lecturer Concepting & Business Innovation at Fontys ILS

In the last decades a range of trend programs emerged from full blown master or bachelor programs to trend modules integrated into curricula and short courses, workshops or webinars on how to research trends. There are also initiatives promoting futures thinking at an early stage and enabling children and youngsters to think about the future in an accessible and playful manner. Teach the Future is one of those initiatives encouraging educators worldwide to integrate futures thinking into school programs.

TEACH THE FUTURE
Erica Bol - Change Maker at Teach the Future

"Teach the Future is a non-profit organisation dedicated to bringing foresight and futures thinking to schools and students around the world. Our goal is to create awareness about the future. We believe that young people of any age can learn to think critically and creatively about the future and develop the agency to influence it. When you think about the future in a conscious way you can steer yourself into a future direction and make choices in the present to get there.

Thinking and talking about the future helps you to understand where you want to go. What you feel is the best possible future depends on all kinds of factors like your age or cultural background. Discussing this with others creates empathy and an understanding that there can be different visions on the future. When talking about the present, people often get stuck in discussions on what's right or wrong. People can think in a more open and free way about the future because there is no right or wrong in something that does not exist yet.

By teaching the future we want to empower people, especially youngsters, and show them that they can be part of change on all kinds of levels, from an individual level to their neighbourhood, their country or the world. By giving young people the tools to engage with the future early in life, we are equipping them to face uncertainties and challenges and helping them discover their role in shaping the future. Prepare students for tomorrow by teaching the future today!"

Although there is no official quality mark for trend researchers, a specific skill set is needed to detect and analyse change. There are some characteristics any trend expert should possess or at least try to cultivate. Take a look at the characteristics list which typifies a good trend researcher.

A trend researcher should be:

» **Curious**: you are eager to absorb knowledge and experiences, you have an inquisitive nature and always wonder about the 'why' of things happening around you. You ask questions more than voicing your own opinions.
» **Non-judgmental**: you have an open minded personality and are able to show empathy. You are unbiased towards opinions and behaviours that differ from your own personal standards. Instead of immediately thinking *'that's not right'*, you think *'that's interesting!'*.
» **Interdisciplinary**: you have a varied skill set involving many areas of knowledge. You can easily think and work across boundaries, combining knowledge from different fields and domains. You have a broad interest and are more of a generalist than a specialist.
» **Holistic**: you look at the bigger picture and how this fits with the details. You can shift from zooming in to zooming out when researching trends. You feel the whole is more than merely the sum of its parts and you do not like to get stuck in the details.
» **Analytic**: you use a structured approach to examine signs of change and operate in a careful, critical and objective way to identify causes and key factors behind shifts. You like to arrange information in an organised way and use a system for this, like colour codes or categories.

- » **Creative**: you are able to see connections between shreds and snippets of information that seem unrelated at first. You can combine these into inspiring and imaginative trend stories.
- » **Persistent**: you are not satisfied easily and want to research beyond the baseline and dive deep into matters. You are not pleased with the first search hit provided by a search engine, you will check other sources to collect more information.
- » **Visual**: you have a flair for visual language and are able to use visual aids to bring your research findings to life. You understand how a picture can demonstrate an abstract shift and you like to work according to the 'show, don't tell' principle.
- » **Recognisable**: you do research in a way that sets you apart from others and leave a personal fingerprint on your reports and presentations. When you use a visual style or write a text, people can identify it as created by you.
- » **Storyteller**: you are able to get your trend story across and adapt it to different audiences without losing your personal touch. You are able to use a combination of words and visuals to create a coherent, logical and inspiring storyline.

"A trend researcher should be sensitive to the spirit of times, work in an organised way and be capable of filtering the most relevant information."

Tessa Cramer - Future-minded Academic and Senior Lecturer Trend Research at Fontys ILS

Do not worry if you cannot check off all of the above characteristics yet. Trend research is not something you can learn by just reading a text book. You will develop the abovementioned skills by practising and you will be given tips and tricks throughout this book to get you started.

QUESTION

Which of the required characteristics do you already possess?
Can you give evidence for this by giving examples from your daily life?

Which of the characteristics do you have to develop more?
How will you try to do this? Think of activities to undertake.

Because of the ongoing developments in the field of trend studies, a very interesting question for a trend researcher is 'what can be possible futures of the trend research profession?'. As someone reading this book and interested in trend research you can be part of the professional development of the trend field. Read more on experts' future visions of the profession in the final chapter of this book.

INTERVIEW | Patrick van der Duin

Patrick van der Duin
*Executive Director at STT and Associate Professor
Futures Research & Trend Watching at Fontys ACI*

What's your vision on the future?

"The future is the only part of our lives we can exert influence on. The past and present are already established, while the future abounds with 'degrees of freedom'. On the other hand I oppose the perspective of a fully open and designable future because we are dependent on others and there are many uncertainties to take into account. I feel the truth lies somewhere between the two visions of a determined and open future."

Can we research the future?

"People often ask me how the future can be researched, because it doesn't exist yet. I always reply: *"Does inflation exist?"* No, it's a social economic construct but it still impacts our society. The same can be said about the future. As a society, we define the notion of a future and to which degree we find it important to think and act on this constructed vision of the future. Therefore the future exists and can be studied."

Why should we research the future?

"To me the main goal of futures research is to provide inspiration for strategic decisions and actions. The research itself is a means to an end and should be action oriented. Research can be focused on the short or long term, but it depends on the heartbeat of the sector you are investigating what short or long is. For instance, what is *long term* for a beverages company like Coca Cola can be *short term* for an energy company like Shell. I feel the crossover point in futures research is much more the level of uncertainty. The moment you feel that you're taking too much risk as a researcher to extrapolate something happening now into the future."

Do you think we can predict the future?

"I always use a disclaimer, because I feel nobody can predict the future. We can try to explore the future, but if you're too much focused on predicting in decimal percentage points you're actually narrowing down the future too much. This type of reasoning doesn't spark any inspiration about the future. For example, big data uses existing data to predict consumers' future behaviour. But it doesn't give way to unexpected variables. Therefore it leans too much on the present instead of opening up our minds about future scenarios. This is exactly why we use creative and imaginative techniques when we build multiple future scenarios, to get detached from the present."

What is the future of researching the future?

"In the future the profession will be headed in the direction of corporate foresight. It will be more about linking futures research to strategy and decision making. Also, we will be investigating preferred futures more. Because so much is possible in our day and age, the main question shifts to if we should want everything that's feasible."

Do you have any tips for readers?

"My advice for aspiring trend researchers is to visit birthday parties, travel by public transport and frequently go grocery shopping. This will help you to stay in touch with nowadays society and give you a reality check."

‹ SUMMARY

» Humans have been fascinated about the future since their existence.

» The purpose of trend research is to detect change, understand why change happens and act upon it to create change.

» Thinking about the future has evolved from prophecy to philosophy to business strategy.

» How you perceive the past affects your present behaviour and this influences your take on the future.

» Trends research is not about predicting the future but about exploring current signs of change and the tracks they provide to alternative futures.

» Trend research as a profession is under construction and finds it roots in various disciplines.

» Trend researchers have a specific skill set that allows them to detect, understand and act on change.

WE
BEAT
THE
FUTURE

‹ WANT TO KNOW MORE?

Eager to learn more about futures studies and trend research? Here you can find some suggestions for further reading, watching and clicking. This is a selection of a vast array of futures oriented networks, universities and books. You can find more information at www.howtoresearchtrends.com.

NETWORKS ··

At the moment there are mainly independent networks of futurists. Networks specifically of trend researchers are not very common yet. There are several events organised around the world dedicated to futures and trend research. You can check the event calendars of the following networks to stay updated on these.

La Futura. A trend and innovation network that aims to bridge the gap between trends, innovation and tomorrow's opportunities. La Futura connects industries and trend experts and is business oriented.

World Future Society (WFS). The World Future Society is a membership organisation in the world for people who research, envision and create potential futures. Their mission is to improve decision making about the future. The WFS also has local chapters, for instance the Dutch Future Society. Check the site to see if your country also has a local chapter.

World Futures Studies Federation (WFSF). The WFSF is a non-profit global NGO that is independent, non-commercial in focus and geared towards strengthening the scholarship of futures research.

Association of Professional Futurists (APF). The APF is a growing community of professional futurists dedicated to promoting professional excellence and demonstrating the value of futures thinking.

Institute for the Future (IFTF). IFTF is an independent, non-profit research organisation helping all kinds of organisations make the futures they want. Their aim is to turn foresight into critical new insights that ultimately lead to action.

The Millennium Project (TMP). The Millennium Project is an independent non-profit global participatory futures research think tank aimed at improving humanity's prospects for building a better future.

EDUCATION

If you want to learn more about the future, you can follow several bachelor or master level studies that incorporate trend research into their curriculum. To name a few:

Creative studies
» International Lifestyle Studies (ILS), Fontys Academy for Creative Industries (ACI), bachelor studies in Tilburg, The Netherlands.
» Universidade de Lisboa, Post-graduate course in Trends Communication in Lisbon, Portugal.
» Strategic foresight and innovation, The Ontario College of Art and Design University (OCAD-U), master studies in Toronto, Canada.
» Trend analysis and implementation, HoGent post-graduate program in Gent, Belgium.
» Trends, specialisation of master studies, Zürcher Hochschule der Künste in Zurich, Switzerland.

Social sciences
» Social foresight, University of Trento, master studies in Trento, Italy.
» Futures Studies, Tamkang University, master studies in Taiwan.
» Futures Studies, University of Hawaii, master studies in Honolulu, Hawaii.

Business studies
» Futures studies, University of Turku, master studies in Turku, Finland.
» Foresight, University of Houston, master studies in Houston, United States.

Teach the Future. A global platform where ideas and materials are shared on teaching the future in primary, secondary and college education.

BOOKS

If you want to do some in-depth reading on future related topics, check out the following books:

» Foundations of Futures Studies volumes 1 & 2 by Wendell Bell
» Teaching the Future by Peter Bishop and Andy Hines
» The Discovery of the Future by Herbert George Wells
» Utopia by Thomas More
» Sociology of Inventions by Seabury Gilfillan
» Future Shock by Alvin Toffler
» The Future is Ours by Graham May
» The Time Paradox by Philip Zimbardo

#2

FRAME WORK

LEARNING THE LINGO
In this chapter you will be introduced to the basic vocabulary and theories used in trend research, including the three core phases of trend studies: scan, analyse and apply. This framework will help you understand and communicate about a trend research process.

☐ TOPICS

☐ INTRO

Hypes, early adopters, trend spots, memes, micro trends, diffusion of innovation, consumer trends, laggards? As in any profession, trend research has its own jargon. It makes it easier for trend researchers to explain, share and discuss their process and findings. However, from an outside perspective it might feel somewhat confusing at first. Even more because trend research is a profession in development and trend researchers themselves do not agree (yet) on which trend terminology to use.

"Credibility is key and this is enhanced by explaining your ways of working. The new school trend approach is about being open and sharing."

Tessa Cramer - Future-minded Academic and Senior Lecturer Trend Research at Fontys ILS

But do not get too distracted by this trend lingo. The main point of this chapter is to become familiar with the various expressions, like a definition of a trend, a theory of change, the trend levels and the basics on values and needs, so you will feel confident in using them yourself. You will be introduced to the basic vocabulary and theories used in trend research on the next pages. It will help you understand the foundation on which the investigation of trends is based and it provides a framework that facilitates your own thinking and communicating about trends.

TREND DEFINITION

The word trend evokes lots of different associations and you might have heard the word trend being used in various ways and in different situations. What are the first thoughts that pop up in your mind when you hear the word trend? And when you ask your family and friends, what type of answers do you get? Experience shows that the way people answer the question 'what is a trend?' can roughly be divided into three categories.

Most people would think a trend is:
» A concrete and specific new manifestation like a fashion style, a novel product or a tech gadget.

Some of them would say a trend is:
» A new attitude, behaviour, need, want or value as seen within certain groups in society, like a focus on eco-friendly consuming or a need for more transparency.

And others would consider that a trend is:
» An on-going worldwide force already happening for several years, like digitalisation or globalisation.

> *"I first thought trends were fashion and interior style related stuff and my initial reaction was: studying trends is not my cup of tea. But as I learned more about it, it made me realise the topic of trends is so much bigger and broader."*
>
> Fleur Stiels - Concept Designer at Dutch Rose Media and former Fontys ILS student

As there is such a wide variety of interpretations of a trend, it is essential to explain which definition of a trend you use as a trend researcher. This way everyone will be on the same page and you will avoid a lot of discussion and confusion.

> *"We define a trend as the general direction of travel of some force. This might sound quite abstract but in essence it is about something going in a specific direction, up or down."*
>
> Sam Shaw - Head of Insight at Canvas8

When you take a peek at the online Oxford Dictionary (2016) it tells you that the definition of a trend is 'a general direction in which something is developing or changing.' But this is still a very broad explanation of a trend. The combination of the three categories of answers mentioned earlier actually define a trend in a more complete manner. A trend integrates all three elements, the manifestations, the underlying needs and wants and the ongoing global forces. The key elements defining a trend are:

» **Direction of change**: when talking about trends, you are talking about the specific direction in which a change you spotted is heading. In which way is it shifting away from the mainstream and the accepted? Is something getting bigger, smaller, going up or down? In this chapter you will learn more about the concept of change.

» **Values and needs**: the direction of change can be pinpointed by describing the specific shift in values and needs, because these define people's attitudes, expectations and mentalities related to the spotted change. In this chapter you will be introduced to theory on values and needs.

» **Forces**: a trend is driven by forces which mainly lie beyond an individual's control and have already been going on for some years, even decades. These forces and drivers should be taken into consideration when researching trends because they are part of a trend's emergence. In this chapter you will be introduced to the STEEP tool to categorise these forces.

» **Manifestations**: the direction of change can be spotted because trends manifest themselves in an observable manner in various ways and across different sectors, for example through language, style, behaviour, products, services, events and movies. Signs of change can be detected by scanning the environment. In chapter three 'Scan' you will get up to speed on how to spot these manifestations of change.

» **Certain groups**: a trend starts within a certain group of people in society before it spreads further and maybe one day becomes accepted and adopted by a majority in society. In this chapter you will learn more about the way change and innovations spread throughout groups in society.

In a nutshell you study change to find patterns that show that people's needs and wants are shifting in certain directions. These patterns of change are called trends. The trends are driven by global forces and already manifest themselves in various ways, like a certain type of style, language, behaviour, a new service or product. These manifestations can be spotted first amongst niche groups in society who are setting the trend or embracing it in an early stage. It is always helpful to have a one sentence definition of a trend to share with your audience. The following sentence combines all aspects of a trend in just one line.

> *A trend is a direction of change in values and needs which is driven by forces and manifests itself already in various ways within certain groups in society.*

This trend definition is the springboard for the remainder of this chapter and throughout this book. See if this definition works for you or tweak it in a way that you feel comfortable working with. The goal is that it helps you to explain your view on trends to others.

> *"We always describe our vision on trends and our research methods upfront. How we describe them depends on who we are talking to, we always adapt it to the people we are working for."*
> Laura Wolfs - Senior Research Consultant at Point Blank International

Trends are often equated to fads and hypes, but there is a distinction. A fad or a craze is a form of collective behaviour that develops within a culture, a generation or any other type of social group and which is followed enthusiastically for a limited period of time. Think of popular fashion styles or specific language deemed cool within a peer group. Fads can fade quickly when the feeling of novelty has gone. A hype is created by advertisers or media to promote a specific idea, event, person or product. The coverage can seem out of proportion to the significance of what is being covered. Think of the hype around a new technological gadget before its official release or the hype around a certain celebrity. For trend professionals, fads and hypes are only interesting in the way that they might be manifestations of a bigger trend and connect with emerging values and needs. This is not always the case and a trend researcher should not get too distracted by passing fads and hypes.

> *"A trend is not a fashion hype, it is a phenomenon that is observable right now which has an impact on a group of people and evokes change."*
>
> Björn Theis - Foresight Manager at Evonik

CHANGE

'The world is changing rapidly'; this phrase is often the first sentence of a trend report or trend presentation, which is not strange because the main research subject of a trend researcher is change. Trend researchers try to think in a systematic way about the future by researching clues of change in the present. By monitoring these observable changes and analysing sources, patterns and causes of change a trend professional makes an educated guess about the impact of the observed change on our future lives.

> *"What interests me is how culture is going to change in the next decades. How will we combine cultural references to create new ones?"*
> Rodrigo dos Reis - Consumer Trends Specialist at Zeitgeist

But what is change exactly? The Oxford Dictionary (2016) states that change is 'an act or process through which something becomes different'.

» Change is an act or process, which implies it is an active modus which you, as a researcher, can observe while it is happening.

» Something goes through this process of change. This something can be tangible things like clothing or food products to intangible elements like ideas, attitudes and opinions.

» This something becomes different. As a trend detective you will have to scan for changes that are different from the current state of affairs, changes that are shifting away from the normal and from accepted behaviours, attitudes and beliefs.

What is the difference in detecting changes with a gut instinct like all humans are genetically wired to do and the way a trend researcher studies change? Your gut detector of change is making you look at your immediate and direct environment only. An unexpected movement seen from the corner of your eye, a strange sound entering your ear. It is in your human genes to pay attention to these things. While most people are paying attention to their immediate environment, trend researchers are also paying attention to the global, macro environment. They connect this with what is happening on a smaller and micro level. What you need to develop is your professional detection of change which also takes into account the bigger picture and looks beyond your immediate surroundings. Trend research is about zooming in and out and in and out over and over again. To study change you will need to be up to date on what is going on in the world on a local as well as a global scale.

> *"There are always new things popping up and you might wonder: have we seen it all now?*
> *But still there are new things coming, they present new challenges and provoke new*
> *uncertainties."*
>
> Sam Shaw - Head of Insight at Canvas8

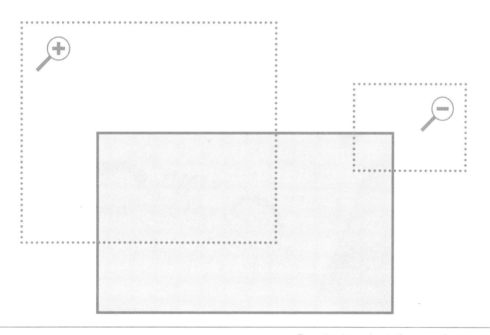

Zooming in and out of your environment.

While most social studies try to investigate human social life in the broadest sense, trend research specifically focuses on the study of change in groups and societies. It studies the spirit of the time while changes are happening instead of looking back on them and analysing change that has occurred.

QUESTION ···

What defines the current zeitgeist?
You are asked to make a movie about the current state of your country. What should definitely be included in this movie? Which social and cultural movements, which icons, which symbols?

Compare your storyline with stories about your country from decades ago. Check movies or drama series from the past about your country. What are similarities and what are differences with the current state of your region?

···

TREND LEVELS

A way of researching change is to break it down into trend levels. Terminology like mega trends, market trends, micro trends, long term trends and consumer trends are all referring to different aspects and levels within a trend. Dissecting change into specific levels helps you to analyse and understand it better, it provides a kind of trend anatomy. As mentioned before there is no consensus on a lot of terminology in the domain of trends and the same goes for the labels of the trend levels. Some trend professionals use a division into mega, macro and micro trends, some use labels like market and consumer trends and others use classifications like short term and long term trends (Dimutrescu, 2012, Roothart, 2002). In the end all categories and labels are aimed at showing that a trend is a build-up of:

» **Manifestations of a trend**: these signals of change are often referred to as the micro, short-term or market trend level. They can have different appearances, ranging from an art object to a commercial service, from a product to a festival. These manifestations can be observed and are evidence that a trend is already happening.

» **Values and needs**: this level is about the underlying values and needs related to the spotted manifestations. It is often referred to as the macro, midterm or consumer trend. This is the core of a trend and shows what the manifestations actually mean to individual people. Think of values and needs like transparency, connectivity and balance.

» **Forces**: this level of a trend is about the forces that are driving the emergence of the trend manifestations and their underlying needs and values. Often referred to as the mega, long term or societal trend level. These forces go beyond the individual's power and slowly, almost unnoticeable, come into people's lives. Think of forces like urbanisation, globalisation and digitalisation.

The levels are interconnected and there is not a linear way of how these are influencing each other. A manifestation, like a 3D printer, is a technological product innovation. But it also shows a need for self-producing and creation and it is driven by forces like digitalisation and globalisation. While doing trend research you are zooming in and out from one level to the other and trying to get an overview of the relations between the levels.

> "Trends come in all shapes and sizes. I'm not interested in gadgets per se, but in the mentality behind the gadgets. These shifting mentalities are placed within the context of forces like economic and political drivers."
>
> Carl Rohde - Culture Sociologist and founder of Science of the Time

The trend levels provide a framework for looking at trends and can be used to analyse and structure the build-up of a trend. Most of the time it is easier for people to understand the full scope of a trend when you show them it is made up of manifestations which relate to emerging values and needs and are driven by societal forces. Chapter four zooms in on analysing a trend and how to integrate these trend levels into your analysis.

> "I see trends as changes in consumer mind-sets. These are often shifts that take a few years to drip down into the mainstream. So while the change in mind-set is a slow shift, keeping up with the manifestations is where we have to go fast."
>
> Pernille Kok-Jensen - Connectivity Director at MARE

FORCES   Digitalisation

↕

VALUES & NEEDS   Creative independency

↕

MANIFESTATIONS   3D printing, open source, creative commons, ...

An example of the trend levels.

FORCES

When investigating a changing environment you can use the STEEP factors to make an inventory of external forces and developments on a local and worldwide scale. STEEP is an acronym that stands for Social, Technological, Economic, Environmental and Political factors. Other acronyms in use are PEST, PESTLE, PESTEL, STEP, DESTEP, PESTO and STEEPLED, adding factors like an L for Legal, E for Ethical, O for Other and D for Demographical. Whichever you use, they are all applied as a memory aid and tool to organise and structure external developments happening in society.

Originally this tool, used since the 1960's, is aimed at helping businesses understand the external environment in which they are operating and the opportunities and threats that lie within it (Francis, 1967). By understanding their environment organisations can take advantage of opportunities and minimise threats. In trend research the STEEP factors are used as a more generic orientation tool to explore and organise what is happening in societies on a local and global scale. You can use it as a checklist to make an inventory of forces of change. The STEEP factors lie mostly beyond the control of individuals in society, it feels like these global developments are happening to us and we are subjected to it. They represent deep structural forces that interact within societies and can create a range of possible futures. Let's take a closer look at each of the STEEP factors.

SOCIAL
Social developments and factors build a society. They influence people's choices and include the beliefs, values and attitudes of a society. These factors include demographics like population growth rate, age distribution, immigration and emigration, living standards and dominant lifestyles. Social factors also include cultural values like health consciousness, religious influence, education and career attitudes, gender diversity and various ethical issues. Consumer behaviour, buying patterns, media views and advertising are social factors too.

Example: driving social forces of change behind the trend of gender bending are, amongst others, the shifts in cultural notions of femininity and masculinity and the way these are portrayed via the media and in advertising.

TECHNOLOGICAL
Technological developments are mainly about studying the rate of technological change and which fields are developing most rapidly by monitoring research and development activities, research funding, licensing and patents, intellectual property issues manufacturing advances, automation and innovation in sectors like transport, energy, health, communication and computing.

Example: technological forces behind the trend of interconnectivity are digitalisation and specifically the rise of internet and mobile technology.

ECONOMICAL
An economic situation is largely related to the buying position of businesses and consumers. Think about factors like interest rates, inflation levels, taxes, debts and savings levels, international trade,

PERSONAL SPACE

PLEASURE

Me-time

INNER HARMONY

CONVENIENCE

INTROVER-

LOHLINESS

men with dogs

economic performance and growth rate, costs of resources, demand and supply models, state of global stock markets, consumer confidence, entrepreneurship and availability of jobs.

Example: driving economic forces behind the recent recession in Western society are, amongst others, shifts in international trade markets and lax monitoring of banks.

ENVIRONMENTAL

Environmental developments include ecosystem factors like water, wind, soil, food and energy. These factors influence and at the same time are determined by the surrounding environment, think of climate, weather, geographical location, environmental offsets, global climate targets and regulations. They are crucial for certain industries like tourism, agriculture and insurances.

Example: driving environmental forces behind the trend of sustainability are heightened awareness of climate change because of change in weather, rise of renewable energy solutions and shifts in attitude towards mass consumption.

POLITICAL

Political factors are concerned with how and to what degree a government intervenes in a society. Governments can have an influence on issues like health, education and infrastructure of a nation. Political developments to watch are policies on tax, fiscals and trade, environmental laws, trade restrictions, funding and grants, lobby and pressure groups, wars and conflicts, leadership and government structures and global levels of political stability. The political landscape can change dramatically because of shifts in power after elections, so keep an eye out for those.

Example: driving political forces behind the trend of transparency are accountability of political powerhouses, a citizen led bottom-up approach of politics and movements revealing political corruption.

> "I always try to understand how technological developments impact more social aspects of life, for instance the evolution of the self, how we form identities and gender questions."
> Laura Wolfs - Senior Research Consultant at Point Blank International

These external factors do not operate separately, they are interrelated and influence each other. For instance social demographics influence environmental issues which in their turn can lead to economic changes and vice versa. You should be up to date on the most important drivers of change at this moment because they are elements of trends and crucial in understanding the context of any trend. In the next chapter 'Scan' you will get tips on how to stay updated.

VALUES AND NEEDS

What do you value most in your life? What are your most urgent needs? These are difficult questions to answer for most people when asked in a direct manner. By investigating manifestations of change trend researchers try to pinpoint shifts in values and needs in a more indirect manner. As a trend detective you need to get to the core of changing values and needs because these define people's changing attitudes, expectations and mentalities. These shifts move beyond the outer layers of products, services or styles and explain why people want to adopt a new kind of behaviour, buy a new product or use a new service.

> *"With trends you should always try to understand the cultural framework in which people live because this frames people's behaviour. Humans don't live isolated lives. I try to understand the system, how it is changing and how this is reflected in the behaviour of people."*
>
> Juan Pablo Zapata Barros - Freelance Trend Researcher

VALUES

A value is a fundamental belief or practice about what is desirable, worthwhile and important to an individual or a society. Values can be held collectively, they lie at the core of all cultures. At the same time every individual can experience and 'colour' a value in their own personal way. Your values become a part of your personality over time and they affect your behaviour. Each culture and each person has different values that guide their daily decision making process. How you spend your money for instance is influenced by what you value. If you value self-development and education then you are likely to save money to go to college, spend money on workshops, training sessions and books.
If you value helping others then you are likely to donate money to charities or support crowd-funding initiatives. If you value spending time with friends you are likely to spend money on going to the movies with them or having dinner.

You obtain values from various sources. For one, the culture you grow up in brings along a certain set of values and tries to instil these on people by rules, rewards and punishments. Also the family unit you grow up in influences your values. You can also observe others demonstrating their values publicly and these people can inspire you and serve as your role model. People combine all these sources to decide which values are most important to them. The ranking of values can change over time, where values do not disappear but are seen as less important at that certain period in time. The nature of changes in values is about re-prioritising rather than replacing. By trying to detect and understand these shifts in values, trend researchers try to uncover emerging values for the coming decade (Bishop, 2012 & Hines, 2011).

> *"Values are representations of end goals, for instance love and happiness. Values can change over time mainly because their meanings and manifestations change throughout time."*
>
> Carlijn Naber - Economic Psychologist and Senior Lecturer Trend Research at Fontys ILS

A model of values widely used is the value framework of social psychologist Milton Rokeach. In his study 'The Nature of Human Values' (1973) he posits that people's opinions and behaviours are influenced by a fixed number of human values. He developed a values classification instrument called the Rokeach Value Survey in which you are asked to arrange 36 values into an order of importance they have to you as guiding principles in your life. Rokeach divided these values into two categories, terminal and instrumental, where the instrumental values are the means to achieve the terminal values. For example, your pursuit of mature love can be an end value in your life. As an instrumental value you might use honesty during your relationship to try to attain mature love in the end.

TERMINAL VALUES refer to desirable end-states of existence. These are the goals that a person would like to achieve during his or her lifetime. These values vary among different groups of people in different cultures.

True Friendship | Mature Love | Self-Respect | Happiness | Inner Harmony | Equality | Freedom | Pleasure | Social Recognition | Wisdom | Salvation | Family Security | National Security | A Sense of Accomplishment | A World of Beauty | A World at Peace | A Comfortable Life | An Exciting Life

INSTRUMENTAL VALUES refer to preferable modes of behaviour. These are preferable characteristics that are a means of achieving the terminal values.

Cheerfulness | Ambition | Love | Cleanliness | Self-Control | Capability | Courage | Politeness | Honesty | Imagination | Independence | Intellect | Broad-Mindedness | Logic | Obedience | Helpfulness | Responsibility | Forgiveness

(Rokeach, 1973)

Rokeach felt that all choices made by people are based upon these values and therefore create the foundation that motivates people over longer periods of time. In trend research you are looking for changes in values, which values are becoming more important and which are becoming less important? You want to understand how this plays out in people's attitudes and behaviour. The Rokeach model can be used as a basis for trend analysis, but you can also use other value systems. The main point is to always move beyond the surface of a manifestation of change and ask yourself: what kind of value does it relate to?

NEEDS

A need is something thought to be a necessity or an essential item required for life. Basic needs are things that are essential to survival, such as food, water, air, shelter and clothing. Needs of people also have a strong influence on people's decision making because they are noted deficits that someone would want to fill immediately. New products, services, styles and behaviours can be a means to fill these needs. Shifts in values also bring along changes in needs. These needs can be categorised in different levels. For instance there are not only material, physical needs such as food or shelter, but also immaterial, psychological needs such as a need for self-esteem. A noted deficit, for example can be that you are thirsty and in need of something to drink. This can be a cold drink, a drink of a certain taste, a drink in a certain bottle and so on, and these specific needs change all the time.

> *"The unmet needs of people are at the core of a trend, because people will always seek ways to fill a gap."*
>
> Kelly McKnight - Head of Culture and Trends at Join the Dots

A need motivates someone to act upon this need. Needs change over time and when one type of need is fulfilled people are motivated to fulfil another level of needs. The task of a trend researcher is, as with values, to monitor which needs are becoming more important and which are becoming less important in a specific society, culture or group of people.

QUESTION

Have your values and needs changed over time?
Values and needs can be quite abstract concepts. To make them come to life, look at them from your own personal perspective.

Check the list of values of Rokeach, which values do you feel are most important to you right now? Have your values changed in priority in the last five to ten years? If so, how come?

Think about material and psychological needs. Which needs do you feel you have right now? Have your needs changed over the last year? If so, how come?

QUALITY OF LIFE

In this book the term quality of life is also used. It refers to people's perception of their position in life in the context of the culture and value systems in which they live and in relation to their goals (WHO, 1997). It is a broad ranging concept influenced in a complex way by a person's different states of wellbeing: physical wellbeing, social wellbeing, mental wellbeing, material wellbeing and their activities and development (Felce, 1995). In the end people want to reach a high quality in life in order to feel happy. Having your needs fulfilled and reaching your end-values is an important part of perceiving a high quality of life. In trend research you can relate to quality of life by asking: is an innovation contributing to a specific aspect of wellbeing? By doing this you can analyse your trend spots in a more meaningful way. Also when applying trends and creating change yourself you can ask yourself: is my innovative idea contributing to other peoples' quality of life?

ADOPTERS OF INNOVATION

How does change spread and innovations become known, popular and adopted? It spreads through people as they share information with each other, which also involves spreading information and opinions about new ideas, behaviours, products and services. If the first adopter of an innovation discusses it with two other people, each of these two passes the new idea along to other peers and so forth. The spread of innovations is often described as a social epidemic, as something contagious that people imitate or adopt. The term 'meme' is also used for this phenomenon. According to biologist Richard Dawkins (1976) a meme is an idea, behaviour or style that spreads from person to person within a culture. He uses the metaphor of a gene to explain that a meme is also a self-replicating unit and can explain cultural evolution and socially learned human behaviour. The adoption of innovations can be seen in the same light. When researching trends you watch this diffusion process closely by observing the people who are spreading and adopting the innovation. This makes it easier for you to understand who the first adopters are and to estimate triggers and barriers for an innovation to spread into the mainstream.

> "Always knock on the doors of creators and innovators and talk about their ideas and visions.
> They are an important source to get early insight into upcoming trends."
>
> Pernille Kok-Jensen - Connectivity Director at MARE

The theory of the diffusion of innovation by sociologist and communication professor Everett M. Rogers, described in-depth in his book Diffusion of Innovations (1962), is still relevant to understand how innovations spread through people. Rogers defines innovation as 'an idea, practice or object that is perceived as new by an individual or other unit of adoption', for instance an organisation. He states that if an idea seems new to an individual, it is an innovation and that the perceived newness of the idea for the individual determines his or her reaction to it. Rogers found that people (and organisations) can be divided into five adopter categories based on their innovativeness, which is the degree in which they are relatively earlier in adopting new ideas than other members of a system. Check the illustration of the adoption curve. As you can see, early in the diffusion process relatively few individuals adopt the innovation. Gradually the rate of adoption speeds up until almost all members of a system adopt the innovation or it dies out somewhere along the curve as innovations can also get rejected because people do not feel the innovation satisfies their values and needs enough.

THE INNOVATION

INNOVATORS	EARLY ADOPTERS	EARLY MAJORITY	LATE MAJORITY	LAGGARDS
2.5%	13.5%	34%	34%	16%

Adopter Categorisation on the Basis of Innovativeness (Rogers, 2003).

What a trend researcher is most interested in is to find out why people create an innovation and why they adopt or reject an innovation. What are their motives, which underlying values and needs emerge when reading about or observing and talking to these people? This helps you in gaining crucial insights for your trend analysis. The five types of adopters defined by Rogers are:

» **INNOVATORS: Venturesome**
These people are willing to take risks and are able to cope with a high degree of uncertainty. They have a high social status and the finances needed to try out innovations. Innovators are social and in close contact to other innovators and sources of innovation like scientific information or inventors. They launch the innovation in a system and have a gatekeeping role in the flow of new ideas into a system. Innovators are a small, niche group of people within a system, only 2.5%.

» **EARLY ADOPTERS: Respect**
These people are opinion leaders who have a high social status within a group. They are respected by members of a system, have an advanced education and are socially forward. Others look at early adopters for advice and information about an innovation, they are the 'go-to' sources and function as role models and influencers. They put their stamp of approval or disapproval on the innovation. They make up 13.5% of a system.

» **EARLY MAJORITY: Deliberate**
This group adopts an idea just before the average member of a system. They provide interconnected-ness in a systems network, because they frequently interact with peers but are not opinion leaders. These people deliberate for some time to adopt an innovation, their decision period takes longer than that of the innovator or early adopter. They have an average social status and are in contact with early adopters but less willing to take risks. This group makes up one third (34%) of a system's population.

» **LATE MAJORITY: Sceptical**
These people are cautious and sceptic about innovations and do not adopt until most others have already done so. Reasons to adopt can be the feeling of peer pressure or economic necessity. They have a below average social status and little financial means, which means they need to know if it is 'safe' to adopt. This group makes up one third (34%) of a system's population.

» **LAGGARDS: Traditional**

This group is the last to adopt an innovation. They are suspicious about innovations and have an aversion against uncertainty. Laggards tend to be conservative and traditional and live within a small social circle which makes them more isolated in a system. They have a low social status and low finances, which makes them extremely cautious in adopting anything new. This group makes up 16% of a system.

Rogers' research found that earlier adopters generally have a higher socioeconomic status, are more empathetic and more able to deal with abstract information than later adopters. They also are more cosmopolitan, look beyond their own culture and feel more in control of their lives and their future. Rogers found no age differences related to the five categories which counteracts the prevalent notion that young people are always earlier adopters. You can also use variations on the model of Rogers, for instance the classification of people into mavens, connectors and salesmen by Gladwell (2002).

You can not only plot people but also organisations and brands on the curve. How sensitive to innovations is an organisation? Are they more of a follower or an innovator? It also defines the 'trend sensitivity' of an organisation. Are they familiar with trends and have they applied them before or are they new in this arena? How do they keep themselves up to date on trends, are they visiting trade shows, reading certain magazines or doing anything else to be informed? When applying trends this is useful information to know, you will read more on this in chapter five.

Because trends are about emerging changes and spotting innovations in an early stage it makes sense to zoom in mainly on the people who spark change: the creators, innovators and early adopters. This does not mean you should ignore the later adopters at all, these adopter types are crucial to investigate to define how difficult or easy it might be to introduce an innovation into a mass market.

QUESTION ···

In which areas are you a frontrunner? In which areas are you a late adopter?
You can be avant-garde in a certain domain but a total laggard in another. Maybe you know everything about gaming but are totally ignorant about fashion? Pick one or more of the following domains and think about your own adopter position in it, are you a frontrunner or a very late adopter?

Automotive / Gaming / Fashion / Food / Beauty / Art / Design / Nightlife / Health / Sports / Technology / ...

···

VARIED LIFE STIMULATION

TREND RESEARCH CYCLE

As a trend researcher you are standing on the crossroads of past, present and future. When trying to make sense of change in the past, present and its possible future consequences you will go through three research phases: scan, analyse and apply. You will be introduced to these research phases right now and dive into them in the next three chapters dedicated to each of these phases. The three phases are related to the goals of trend research:

» **detect**: the scan phase focuses on finding signs of change
» **understand**: the analyse phase relates to understanding the signs of change
» **act**: the apply phase is about implementing trend insights to create change

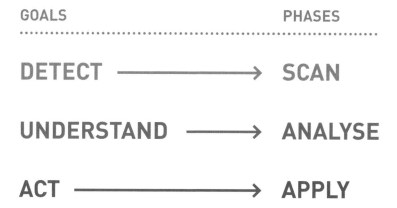

The three phases are quite generic and applicable for any kind of research project, not just trend research. However, the way trend researchers execute these phases makes it stand out from other types of research, for instance market research. The process itself is certainly not very black-and-white divided into these three phases, but is dynamic, ongoing and iterative. While scanning, you might already analyse signs of change and think of ways to act upon it. For the sake of understanding how trend research works, the process has been split up into these three separate phases.

> "I always explain trends by saying that the only constant is change. So if change is a constant factor you should monitor it, which is an ongoing and never ending process."
> Claudia Lieshout - Creative Director Lifestyle Trends at Philips Design

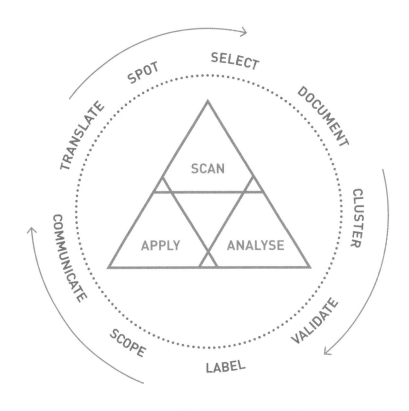

The trend research cycle.

» **SCAN: the art of looking sideways**

The future is happening right now. How do you find these manifestations of the future? In this phase you will practice the art of looking sideways by scanning the environment for seeds of change. Scanning the world means having your radar on always, anytime, anywhere. The scanning process is not done at random. Trend researchers scan the environment using various sources which can mainly be divided into two categories:

» Field research sources like street hunting, innovator interviews and attending events
» Desk research sources like reading magazines, monitoring online media and watching documentaries

In chapter three you can read more about different ways of scanning for change.

» **ANALYSE: connecting the dots**

One manifestation of change is not yet a trend. While scanning you collect a lot of information and making sense of your findings is the next phase of the trend research process. In this phase you will move from trend spots to underlying shifts in values and needs. You will uncover patterns between manifestations and turn these into meaningful clusters of trends and describe and visualise these in an inspiring way for others to understand too. In chapter four you will be informed on how to analyse your trend spots.

» **APPLY: innovate or die!**
The analysis phase will result in an overview of several trends. The next step is to decide on which trends to apply and integrate them into innovation processes with a specific scope. This all depends on the goals of the organisation that wants to apply trend insights. In chapter five you will read more about defining a scope, deciding on a communication approach and how to take the first steps into translating your trends in a tailor-made way so they can be applied as a springboard for innovation.

QUALITATIVE APPROACH
The trend research method described in this book is mainly focused on qualitative ways of doing research. This is the type of research where you collect information in a systematic way about situations, events and people by going out into the world and try to get in-depth understanding of human behaviour by for instance observing and talking to people. Qualitative research also takes into account the totality of a situation and offers a holistic view on any topic. As a qualitative trend researcher you should always want to understand the 'why' behind manifestations of change and what they mean to people.

The 'why' is often not expressed in numbers but through visual and verbal information. The way of trend researching explained in this book uses only partly a quantitative approach, mostly via secondary sources found via desk research. The aim of finding and using these numbers is to substantiate your qualitative findings. Qualitative research is subjective, you are taking your own perspective into the research as you interact with events and persons. As a researcher you have to be aware of this and self-reflect on it from the very beginning of your research process. Therefore it is always crucial to discuss and cross reference your findings with others to validate your trend story.

> *"Always try to take a neutral standpoint, don't dismiss things because you feel like that people voicing certain opinions are stupid or ignorant. Try to stay objective and don't think too much in terms of good or bad."*
>
> Valeria Ossio - Service & Strategic Designer at Mandalah

EMOTIONAL OR RATIONAL
The way trend researchers execute their research process differs in their focus on a more emotional approach or on a more rational approach.

A slider between the emotional and rational.

The emotional approach is a more intuitive, visual and creative way of doing research where you would use all your senses, do mainly field research and integrate a lot of visual material. The rational approach is a more factual, analytic and text based way of doing research where you would do mainly desk research, use a lot of renowned sources and also look for numbers and figures to show that a development is happening right now. Not one approach is 'the best' one. It all depends on how well you execute your research anyway, whether it is more emotional or more rational focused. Most trend researchers tend to be somewhere in the middle of these two approaches and combine the visual and creative aspect with expert opinions, facts and figures. Experiment with your research on both sides of the spectrum and get a feel for which approach suits you best, the emotional or the rational?

QUESTION ··

What is the research process of trend professionals?
Do some desk research on a couple of trend professionals, check out their website and their trend stories. How do they describe their research process and the methods they use? Can you position them on the emotional-rational scale?

··

There is no fixed formula in doing trend research and trend professionals have different approaches to carrying out their research. But as this chapter showed you, it is helpful to use a framework to base your trend research process on. Now it is time to get yourself into action mode because you will learn the most by doing. The next three chapters will guide you through the three trend research phases and will provide you with a lot of activities to explore and find out what works best for you.

INTERVIEW | Carlijn Naber

Carlijn Naber
Economic Psychologist and Senior Lecturer Trend Research at Fontys ILS

Why do you teach trend research?
"I love to share knowledge and especially like to show students the added value of understanding the why behind shifts in values and needs and how trends insights can be used as input in a creative process. In the end I want students to create products and services that help people to make more sensible decisions and create a more equal society."

What's your vision on the trend research process?
"I feel it's important that trend research doesn't work according to a fixed formula because it forces you to investigate your own choices in setting up your research and to look for exciting and new ways in detecting and analysing trends. Having a flexible research approach and working in a multidisciplinary way creates the best circumstances to execute trend research. That's why I provide my students with a basic framework but not a trend formula to fill in."

What is the added value of a structured process?
"The trend research process should have a solid foundation. As a researcher you should be able to demonstrate that a trend pattern you're observing is based on credible sources and can be put in a context, for instance a specific culture or mentality group. This helps in making your research clear and understandable for others."

What is the foundation of trend research?
"The body of knowledge for trend research at our academy is social studies and its research methodologies. We use mostly qualitative methods, knowledge about systems thinking and theories about human behaviour. Because meanings and manifestations of values change over time they also evoke new needs. In trend research it is important to explain the change in underlying values and needs very clearly because it forms the core of your trend analysis."

Can you give an example of changing values and needs?
"Being healthy used to be about your body physically working. A need would be to have a prosthesis when having a malfunctioning limb. Nowadays being healthy is also about a balance in body and soul. Which for instance creates a need to fight phantom pain and increases the importance of studying your brain and how it interconnects with your body. In the future being healthy might be about becoming the perfect human. A need might be to upgrade yourself in various ways from a robotic arm to implementing a brain chip."

Do you have any advice for readers?
"When you want to cultivate a broader orientation on the world you should approach this as an ongoing process rather than a periodical add-on. So feed yourself on the world out there. It is impossible to stay updated on everything, but at least try to surprise yourself sometimes in the sources you use to develop yourself as a trend researcher. This will also help you in finding your own interests and niche in the trend field."

□ SUMMARY

» There is no fixed vocabulary that all trend professionals use.

» A trend is a direction of change in values and needs which is driven by forces and manifests itself already in various ways within certain groups in society.

» Change is the main research subject of trend researchers and zooming in and out on change is essential.

» Trend manifestations, values and needs and driving forces are levels within a trend.

» STEEP is a tool to make an inventory of forces that play out beyond the individual's control.

» Emerging values and needs are at the core of a trend and change over time.

» Creators, innovators and early adopters are the type of people to watch closely.

» The trend research process consists of three phases: scan, analyse and apply.

» The research process in this book has a mainly qualitative approach and has an iterative and dynamic character.

☐ WANT TO KNOW MORE?

Are you eager to learn more about the theoretical framework of trend research? Here you can find some suggestions for further reading, watching and clicking. This is a selection of a vast array of trend books, documentaries and other sources. You can find more information at www.howtoresearchtrends.com.

BOOKS ON TREND RESEARCH ···

- » The Trend Forecaster's Handbook by Martin Raymond
- » Road trip to Innovation by Delia Dumitrescu
- » Trend-driven Innovation by Henry Mason, David Mattin, Maxwell Luthy and Delia Dumitrescu
- » Anatomy of a Trend by Henrik Vejlgaard
- » Fashion Forecasting by Evelyn L. Brannon
- » The Trend Management Toolkit by Anne Lise Kjaer
- » Foresight in Organizations, edited by Patrick van der Duin
- » Diffusion of Innovations by Everett M. Rogers
- » The Tipping Point by Malcolm Gladwell
- » Consumer Shift by Andy Hines
- » Big Bang Disruption by Larry Downes and Paul Nunes.
- » Mastering the Hype Cycle by Jackie Fenn and Mark Raskino
- » Transformations by Grant McCracken

VIDEOS ON TREND RESEARCH ···

- » Influencers: how trends and creativity become contagious, directed by Paul Rojanathara and Davis Johnson
- » Trend Beacons, directed by the Markell brothers
- » V for Vendetta: you cannot kill an idea, directed by James McTeigue

TOOLS ···

- » The Gartner Hype Cycle for Emerging Technologies
- » Mind the Future box, a compendium for contemporary trends packed within a box.

#3

SCAN

THE ART OF LOOKING SIDEWAYS
The future is starting and happening right now. How do you find manifestations of the future? This chapter is about the art of looking sideways. You will read loads of tips and tricks on how to make a scan plan to source your surroundings for seeds of change.

≡ TOPICS

= INTRO

One of the goals of trend research is to detect change. To find signs of change you will have to scan your environment continuously. As a trend researcher your life is never on pause and your radar is on: always, anytime and anywhere.

> *"You need to surround yourself with all kinds of stimuli and make being up to date part of your day-to-day life. I don't think you can be a part-time trend researcher because you need to update and refresh your brain all the time."*
>
> Kelly McKnight - Head of Culture and Trends at Join the Dots

In this chapter you will practice the art of looking sideways (Fletcher, 2001) and be introduced to a three step approach of scanning. The first step is to spot signs of change using desk research and field research activities. Then you will practice making a first selection of your trend spots based on a list of criteria. And finally, you will find a fitting way to describe and archive these selected spots in a trend database.

OBSERVE

Everybody looks at the world in their own specific way, which becomes habitual and can be hard to adjust. Before diving into the three-step process of scanning, let's first reflect on the most important tool in scanning: observing. When you want to scan your environment for change, you need to be able to direct your gaze beyond the usual. You need to start observing in ways you never did before. Looking sideways is needed to avoid looking in just one direction. Or, as trend expert Faith Popcorn (1992) puts it, you have to engage in 'Cultural Brailling': *"Scan today's culture for signs of the future. I think of this as brailling the culture, reaching out to touch as many parts of it as possible - to make sense of the whole. Compensating for tunnel vision by developing a different sensitivity, a "feel" for what's going on."*

It is no wonder that the label trend 'watcher' has come into vogue, because watching, observing and looking is an important part of the job. To become an excellent trend scanner you will need to have an eye for detail as well as a helicopter view. So activate your antenna and use all your senses to soak up what is going on right now in society. Shifts can emerge from unexpected places, so it is essential that you observe across domains, cultures and lifestyles. If you are working in the health sector you should also observe what is happening outside your domain, for instance in the food sector or the leisure field. Trends and their underlying values transcend industry borders and often manifest themselves throughout several domains at the same time in different shapes and forms. Looking into other sectors provides useful information regarding emerging trends. For the same reason you should also look across borders and not only spot in your own home town, region or culture but also outside of these. Travel a lot to seek signs of change. The same goes for spotting across lifestyles, always be on the look-out for anything new in various mentality groups in society.

"When spotting trends we cast the net very wide and cover a number of different markets and sectors because we work for such different clients."

Sam Shaw - Head of Insight at Canvas8

SCAN STEPS

When you are told to 'just' start scanning and look around you, you might wonder where to start. There are various ways to scan and these can assist you in broadening your view. To help you get started and scan in a structured way, the scanning process is divided into three steps: Spot, Select and Document. On the next pages you will dive into every step and understand how to use these to create the foundation of your trend database.

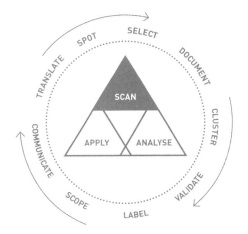

STEP 1: SPOT →

Scanning starts with spotting signs of change. You need to collect evidence that shifts are taking place. It is essential during this step to spot as much as you can across a wide range of subjects. Quantity goes above quality in this step of the research process. In this part you will be brought up to date on various ways of spotting.

STEP 2: SELECT →

From your pile of trend spots you first make a rough selection and cherry pick the most relevant signs. As opposed to spotting, quality goes above quantity during selecting. This segment will show you which criteria to use to choose the most relevant spots.

STEP 3: DOCUMENT

You really need to know every selected trend spot back to front. During this step you will enrich your selected spots and create a detailed description of each one. Lastly, documenting also includes filing all your findings in a way you can retrieve them easily again. In this section you will read about ways of describing your spots and systems for archiving.

STEP 1: SPOT

The first step in the scan phase is to start spotting manifestations of change. As mentioned earlier in chapter one, the characteristics of a trend researcher are to be open, curious and non-judgmental. Your ground attitude as an observer of change should be that everything can be interesting. The challenge lies in postponing your own personal judgment and opinion at first. When you feel that you find something weird, very beautiful or disgusting, always ask yourself: why does it make me feel this way? Spotting trends will learn you a lot about your own specific ways of observing the world and helps you to broaden your horizon.

> "You need to be conscious of your own point of view. Which things do you notice and how do you feel about these? How would others feel about it? This will help you to observe from a third-person perspective. You need to take the role of the observer, become a fly on the wall."

Djenny Brugmans and Nanon Soeters - Partners at Rozenbrood

Remember, you are not just spotting at random, you are looking for signs that relate to change. It must be something new, happening right now that can be observed. New means it has to be different from what is normal and accepted by most people within a society. Signs of change run against current and conventional thinking. These signs might be weak signals and seem like random noise, but when you practice the art of looking sideways you will get more sensitive to change and pick upon these signals quicker and easier. Go for quantity during this step and try to find as many clues of change as you can. A lot of similar signs can show a pattern of emerging values and needs and point in the direction of a trend.

QUESTION

Can you look through different glasses?
To practice switching point of views and put on the perspective of different types of people, try to think in the following way about your trend spots.

What would my ..... [insert person, for example: sister | grandpa | father | neighbour | mailman .....] think about ..... [insert trend spot .....]?

There are many different ways to collect information. As mentioned in chapter two, this book is focused on a qualitative approach of doing trend research. The main qualitative methods of trend spotting can be categorised into field research and desk research activities. Field research for instance can include conducting interviews with frontrunners or observing innovative locations. Desk research can include analysis of existing documents, like blogs, newspaper articles, documentaries and so on. The best way to spot change is to combine various research activities and methods which is called 'triangulation' in research terminology. On the following pages you will be introduced to various ways of executing field and desk research in order to spot signs of change. It is not enough to only read about these activities, you really should try them out. Before you start running to your front door or computer, first consider the following: are you going to spot with or without a focus?

> *"In trend research you don't know upfront what you are looking for. You need to dive in with an open mind and start exploring."*
>
> Kelly McKnight - Head of Culture and Trends at Join the Dots

When you are starting out in trend research you have a clean slate. You have to build up your trend archive from scratch. This often means you have no clear focus in spotting. To make it easier, you can start by spotting in a domain you are already interested in or focus on the topic of a project you are currently working on. If you find it easier to define a specific scope first, then check the section on this in chapter five.

> *"If you have no clue where to begin, start with what really bothers or interests you."*
>
> Niels van der Burg - Global Category Insights Manager at Asics

FIELD RESEARCH

What kind of changes do you see happening in society when you look around you? This is the main question and starting point of spotting via field research. While online research is a great way to gather information from around the world, it is still only one way to collect material. As change can manifest itself anywhere, you should scan multiple sources to gather a diverse set of trend evidence. Doing field research is about exploring in a five dimensional way and using all your senses, not just your eyes. It is crucial for your research to easily switch these sensors on. So before you even set foot outside your door, you should activate and prepare your senses first. Learn from the best, for instance from the inspiring smell expert Sissal Toolas on using your nose. Just like Tolaas does yoga every morning to keep her body fit, she does a 30-minute workout each day for her nose, keeping her sense of smell sharp (Delaney, 2016). Plugging and unplugging her nose is part of this routine. *"My nose has become very important for me to understand the world. You have this device on your body and you just have to use it and it's free. It's there for a purpose, and we have forgotten it."*

QUESTION ··

What are you sensing?

» Which of your senses do you use the most?
Why these and how do you use them?

» Which of your senses do you need to develop more?
Why are these not activated yet?

···

You can stimulate your senses by doing some simple exercises. There are various books available to train your sensory skills like 'How to Become an Explorer of the World' or 'The Modern Day Spotter's Guide'. It often helps to leave the familiar and known to open up your senses, that is why travelling or getting lost are great ways to get out of your comfort zone and open up.

"Wake yourself up and stimulate your senses, go on a field trip and do something you have never done before."

Djenny Brugmans and Nanon Soeters
- Partners at Rozenbrood

INTERVIEW | Zuzanna Skalska

Zuzanna Skalska
Founding Partner of 360 Inspiration

Which trade shows do you visit?
"I visit a lot of trade shows all over the world. I always try to cover eight different industries: home, consumer electronics, packaging, public spaces, transportation, food, medical systems and professional tools."

Why do you visit trade shows?
"By visiting these fairs constantly year after year I have created a huge collection of signals in these eight domains. This enables me to evaluate what is happening, how the domains change and evolve. I always visit press conferences during these fairs, because that is where I hear why companies and brands are making a change. This is crucial in understanding the signs you spotted at the shows. Also, these trade shows are very good for connecting with business professionals and expanding your network."

How do you prepare for a trade show visit?
"You should always find out beforehand who the leading brands are at these shows and prepare a list of must-see brands. Study the floor-plan of the fair upfront and check out which companies are in which halls and decide on the halls to visit and which to skip. Prepare questions you want to ask the exhibitors.

How do you actually visit a trade show?
"To really experience a trade show you should spend a whole day there, from opening to closing time. You should make a lot of pictures and talk to a lot of people. This way you experience the vibe and the overload of information. You will learn by doing because for sure you will make mistakes at first, such as skipping an important hall or taking the wrong kind of pictures. Visiting shows will teach you how to look and how to take your own type of pictures.

"To really experience a trade show you should spend a whole day there, from opening to closing time."

What do you do with all the trade show information?
"After a visit to a trade fair you might feel overwhelmed and not yet know what you have seen really is about. Print out all your pictures and make clusters to define the DNA of the trade show. After this analysis you might catch the fair virus and want to visit shows again and again."

QUESTION ···

Can you activate your senses?
Doing some small, low-key exercises can help you to unlock your senses. Try the following ones that you can do in or outside your home:

» Look in other directions than usual. For instance, look at the ground, what do you see?

» Zoom in. For example, try to spot yellow objects around you.

» Tune into a specific sense. Close your eyes and inhale smells or listen to sounds around you. What are you noticing?

» Take a train or bus you have never taken before. How does this makes you feel?

» Go out for dinner on your own. What are you sensing?

» Buy your groceries at a different store than normally. What stands out?

Now that you have woken up your senses, it is time to focus your field research on not just spotting random things but seeds of change. Many find it difficult at first to start looking for the next and the new. Because when is something really new or just new to you? But you will have to start somewhere to train your feeling for newness and build a frame of reference. Here are some suggestions for field research sources to look for when you hit the streets:

FIELD RESEARCH SOURCES

FRONTRUNNERS
The creators, innovators and early adopters are important sources of information when you want to spot change. You need to find them, talk to them and uncover their drivers for creating or adopting change. This can be done by a formal in-depth interview or an informal chat on any of the below mentioned locations. You can read more on how to find these people in the last paragraph of the Spot section.

AREAS
Visit interesting areas in your city, region, country or abroad. These areas are mostly off the high streets and revolve around upcoming neighbourhoods which are often situated at the fringes, where people flock because space and housing is still affordable. Think of upcoming areas in your own city or region: which areas could you pay a visit?

LOCATIONS
Visit inspiring and innovative locations, from creative hubs to new types of shops, bars, restaurants or any other lifestyle related locations. Many city blogs or magazines showcase the latest interesting venues. Have you been to that new store you drove by last week? Have you checked that new urban space that opened recently?

STREETS
When walking around from one location to another also pay attention to the streets you are walking on, what story do they unveil? For instance:
» Check stickers on traffic lights and lampposts. These objects can be cluttered with sticky messages that contain interesting expressions of activists.
» Graffiti or street art in public spaces show topics certain people want to draw attention to.
» Posters and other notices provide clues on visual aesthetics and emerging themes.
» Window shopping is also relevant because the design of these windows can inform you about emerging visual styles.
» And last but not least, observe the people in the streets, how are they behaving, what are they wearing?

> "I'm always on the lookout for graffiti in strange places. Street artists are often politically involved people with an opinion written in a language that I understand."
> Pernille Kok-Jensen - Connectivity Director at MARE

FLYER HUNTS
Racks with flyers, piles of leaflets, free papers and magazines are there to get ransacked. Fill your bag with any of these you come across and inspect them later at home in more detail. Flyers can inform you about interesting events and festivals to visit, websites to check, interesting expressions and visual shifts.

EXHIBITIONS

Visit museums and exhibitions where works of upcoming and established artists are shown. The topics they address and the way they address these, whether via a painting, a sculpture or an installation, give you a glimpse into emerging themes in society. Also visit graduation shows of art and design academies to be updated on issues explored by a young generation.

> *"Creatives and designers have great antennas for receiving upcoming trends and are the first to give a shape to these trends. Creating is their tool to communicate their message to the world. If you learn their language you are always one step ahead."*
>
> Djenny Brugmans and Nanon Soeters - Partners at Rozenbrood

EVENTS

Debates, lectures, talks, seminars, project presentations, book launches, opening parties, any events where interesting and innovative people voice their opinion are worth checking out. Always explore various events and immerse yourself in different scenes. Go to a technology inspired event and to a fashion show. Check out an academic event as well as an artsy one. Visit events in and outside of your hometown to broaden your scope. Drop in on high paced events with short talks, like a Pecha Kucha, and frequent in-depth debates that go on for hours. You will be amazed how many of these you can attend for free or just a small fee. Sometimes events provide a live stream so even the most diehard couch potato does not have an excuse to not virtually visit an event.

> *"I visit conferences on different topics such as seminars of futurist societies, Ted talks and events about arts, electronica, natural science and digital technology like the World Web Forum."*
>
> Björn Theis - Foresight Manager at Evonik

FESTIVALS

Visit various music, art and theatre festivals, from underground to more mainstream ones. When you are there always observe the people attending and their behaviour, what's there to see, hear, eat and buy? Which brands are present at festivals and in what way?

TRADE SHOWS

Trade shows and fairs are industry exhibitions where companies in a specific domain can showcase their latest products and services. Visiting trade shows is handy to get an update of the status quo within a specific domain, whether it is fashion, food, games or cars. Just to name a few, Paris Fashion week, the CES, a consumer electronics show held in Las Vegas, the Salone de Mobile, an interior design show organised in Milan, SEMA, an automotive trade show and so on. It is impossible to visit them all, but you can check the website of the trade shows to get a feel of the programme and use social media feeds to stay updated on activities during the trade shows from the comfort of your own home.

FIELD RESEARCH POINTERS

Whether you are attending an event or visiting an upcoming neighbourhood, the following tips and tricks are applicable for any kind of field research activity.

GO-TO SOURCES

To find out where to go you can use various sources like city blogs or city event calendars, newsletter subscriptions of event locations, platforms of interests groups and social media event calendars. Combine the input of these sources to create your own personalised event calendar.

RECORD EVERYTHING

You probably do not have photographic memory, so take pictures, record video, take notes and describe the signs of change you have spotted. You can also instantly upload your field research findings in filing tools and apps.

> "During field research I really had to train myself in making notes about the photos I took, such as where it was taken and how I felt about the object photographed. Because when I got home I always forgot these things."
>
> Magė Fledžinskaitė - Former exchange student at Fontys Minor Trend Watching

WHAT'S IN YOUR BAG?

When you are on the go, be prepared for unforeseen circumstances and carry equipment in your bag. From electronic equipment like a camera or extra battery to practical stuff like an umbrella, food and business cards to hand out.

> "I try to be an extreme light packer because I like to walk a lot. I have a back pack and usually carry a small laptop, smartphone, compact camera, multi-tool, lots of pens, a bottle of water and a box for food on the go."
>
> Rodrigo dos Reis - Consumer Trends Specialist at Zeitgeist

GO ALONE

To really immerse yourself into your surroundings you should do your field research alone. This way you do not get distracted by chit chat of others and are more in touch with the world around you. It also allows you to be more open to talk to strangers and mingle with people who can be valuable sources of information.

DESK RESEARCH

What seeds of change can you spot when scanning existing information? This is the main question and starting point of your desk research. From scientific journals to lifestyle blogs, from newspapers to podcasts, you are surrounded by innovative inspiration already put into words or images by someone else. You can take the word desk in desk research quite literal, and think about all the information available to you by just sitting behind your desk and flicking on your laptop, TV, opening a book or a magazine. Going online to research is a great way to gather free information from around the world. But do not only linger online, also check out your local library and bookstores and use various desk research sources.

The quality of your desk research depends very much on your search techniques and skills. It requires you to have an extensive vocabulary to formulate keywords and think in creative ways about where and how to find interesting sources of information. Online tutorials can help you to master search techniques, for instance 'become a power searcher' by Google or tutorials created by public libraries. It is crucial to stay critical during a search and not be satisfied with a first hit. Experiment with using alternative keywords and synonyms, you can find these by using a thesaurus.

QUESTION ··

Can you experiment with search queries?
When you are asked to find, for instance, the latest innovations in the domain of health, which keywords would you use to kick off an online search?

Discuss with others and get inspired to use other keywords.
Adjust your search query by typing in different keywords separately or combined and evaluate the results.

···

Another useful skill in desk research is to be able to scan through pages and documents fast and skim the surface for relevant information. The faster you can read, the less time consuming your desk research will be. To train this you can find many books and tutorials on speed reading. Be aware of your preference in desk research sources. You probably have your go-to sources, like a magazine you always buy or a blog you always check. And maybe you also have specific sources you avoid and never read or watch? It is crucial to expand your view and use a variety of desk research sources for spotting manifestations of change. Only then you can gain a multifaceted overview of what is going on in the world around you.

> *"Before you start reading, be aware that you are influenced by everything you read. Ask yourself: Why am I reading this? What is my perspective? Understand your own point of view."*
> Franklin Ozekhome - Pop Culture Strategist at TINK

Here are some suggestions for desk research sources to look for when you sit at your desk:

DESK RESEARCH SOURCES

BOOKS
Whether non-fiction or novels, any book that shows a future perspective can be a source of inspiration. Frontrunners write about their vision within their area of expertise, for instance about the future of the planet, the future of gender or the future of the internet. Novels can also be a source of inspiration and fuel your imagination about possible future worlds. These books do not always need to be brand new because their content can stay relevant for a longer period of time. Ask friends, colleagues, fellow students or teachers for advice on what to read, check the book sections in papers and magazines or the reading lists of trend professionals.

> "You can call me old fashioned but I really value reading books and my clients value it too. These books embody the knowhow of great experts and visionaries who take a deep dive into a specific topic and get to the bottom of it."
>
> Carl Rohde - Culture Sociologist and founder of Science of the Time

NEWS MEDIA
Make sure to switch newspapers every now and then so you read different ones which voice all kinds of opinions, from financial ones to foreign ones. Besides the traditional newspapers also tune into national and international online news sources too. Also read free newspapers handed out at locations like public transport sites.

MAGAZINES
Visit your local newsstand or go online to check out interesting national and international magazines. From lifestyle oriented ones to domain focused ones, from popular ones to more underground and niche magazines. You can find free magazines too in stores, flyer racks and online.

> "I read opinion-making papers and magazines, like Time, Newsweek, Fast Company, Harvard Business Review, The Guardian, The New York Times, Forbes and The Financial Times. In all these sources you can find information about movements in different business sectors, about who is hired, who is fired, who is going bankrupt and who is buying other companies."
>
> Zuzanna Skalska - Founding Partner of 360Inspiration

SCIENTIFIC JOURNALS
Slightly more difficult to read for most but certainly an interesting source of information are scientific journals. These are published multiple times a year for various academic domains, from technology to culture. You can find these via academic platforms like ResearchGate or use specific search engines like Google Scholar. If academic writings are not your cup of tea you can try shortcuts, like reading interviews with academics in newspapers and magazines or watch videos where academics talk about their findings in a more accessible way.

"One starting point is to check which research topics are popular right now and where research money is allocated to. Because new research findings may lead to new developments fuelling new trends."

Björn Theis - Foresight Manager at Evonik

TV

It is alright to hang out in front of your TV once in a while because it is part of your desk research. Switch on your screen and watch a specific documentary, news show or human interest program. Check commercial and public broadcasters, watch regional, national and international shows. Or randomly flick through channels once a month to stay updated on the media landscape. And do not go to the toilet when the commercials air, because these can give you a feel about advertising aesthetics and sentiments.

"I love the commercials of the year awards because they explain in an insightful way why the commercials won, taking into account the innovative communication factors and how consumers absorb these types of commercials."

Niels van der Burg - Global Category Insights Manager at Asics

MOVIES AND SERIES

Movies and series can provide interesting perspectives on our present day lives by showing future scenarios, from drama to action to science fiction. Watch a movie or series regularly to spark your imagination. Script writers often do extensive research to fuel interesting realistic future scenarios.

DOCUMENTARIES

To become acquainted with various topics you can also watch documentaries. These are aired on TV, can be found online or are showcased at documentary festivals around the globe. The great thing about documentaries is that they show results of in-depth research into a specific topic in an accessible way and often include interesting interviews.

TED TALKS

TED is a platform devoted to spreading ideas in the form of videos of short talks at conferences by visionaries and experts from various disciplines and cultures. TED covers many topics from science to business to global issues in a multitude of languages. TED talks are a great way to be updated on a certain expert vision within a short timeframe.

BLOGS AND VLOGS

These regularly updated sites edited by individuals and published in an informal style are great sources of inspiration about any kind of topic. Ranging from tutorials in business modelling to sharing the newest in gaming, you can select bloggers or vloggers to follow who provide you with relevant information.

CROWDFUNDING PLATFORMS

You can find all sorts of crowdfunding platforms online, from national to international, from domain specific to mixed ones. These platforms showcase bottom-up oriented projects that people feel might be interesting for others to invest in. Besides quirky hobbyist projects you can surely find some interesting, innovative projects on these platforms.

FIGURES AND STATS

Although this book mainly focuses on qualitative trend research, numbers can be very helpful in validating your qualitative trend insights. You do not have to develop your own surveys, you can find loads of secondary data via desk research. The most interesting data types to check are monitors and prognoses because they show that something is or might be changing in the future. Sources you can use are national or international statistics institutions or commercial reports by commercial market analysis agencies. Often they provide a service to subscribe to that keeps you up to date on the latest reports.

> *"With some corporate clients I need quantitative data to back my trend analysis. With demographic data or sector specific numbers I make my own 'sculpture' of numbers."*
>
> Rodrigo dos Reis - Consumer Trends Specialist at Zeitgeist

TREND PLATFORMS

Trend agencies and trend professionals often share snapshots of their trend insights for free on their trend platforms. You can gather trend information by following these and use, for example, a manifestation found on a trend blog in your own trend presentation. The unwritten rule is never to copy-paste someone else's trend analysis without crediting the author. Students in trend research often have blogs where they share findings and projects that might be worthwhile following.

SOCIAL MEDIA

Social media platforms are also interesting portals of information and are great for finding seeds of the new. Whether because experts post something innovative in the platforms news feed or to get a feel about the general public's reactions to certain kinds of innovative topics. Since these platforms tend to emerge and fade over the years, you should move with these platforms.

> *"I screen the media environment to see which type of posts are shared and reposted in local social media. This tells me a lot about short term trends in communication."*
>
> Ksenia Penkina Lery - CEO of Trendsquire

PODCASTS

Listening to podcasts series is also a time efficient way to do desk research, because you can listen while commuting or before you doze off to sleep. It is easy to use on the go by downloading a podcast app on your mobile device. There is a wide range of formats available from in-depth interviews to more snackable content covering a wide range of topics.

DESK RESEARCH POINTERS

Whether you are reading a newspaper or listening to a podcast, the following tips and tricks are useful for any type of desk research activity.

SEARCH ENGINES

Online search engines are a great tool to search in a focused way for specific topics or people. Search engines offer various ways to look for information and refine your search criteria, such as text, images or video. As mentioned earlier it all comes down to training your search skills. Be aware that search engines adjust their search results to your online behaviour which might lead you to get stuck in your own filter bubble. Try various search engines and, if possible, on different devices.

SNOWBALLING

In most desk research sources experts and innovators are cited so you keep 'snowballing' into new information and interesting people. You can dissect interesting quotes from articles and use these as signals of change too. To keep the ball rolling try to find out what these experts use as their favourite sources of information or what they are reading at the moment.

LANGUAGES

It is useful if you master more than one language, this way you can harvest information from more sources. Even if you are not fluent in another language it can pay off to search using this other language and find hidden gems of information.

BOOKMARKING

Besides creasing the corners of book pages you can use digital tools to bookmark interesting sources of information to remind you of to-read articles or file information. From making a favourites lists via a browser to using RSS feeds or apps.

> *"I personally use an RSS feed system for over three hundred different sources. Checking it randomly can be quite overwhelming, so I use it mainly when I already have an idea or topic in mind and search for related information in the RSS feed. This is an easy and good way to monitor weak signals and emerging issues."*
>
> Björn Theis - Foresight Manager at Evonik

SOCIAL MEDIA DASHBOARDS

It is a hopeless task to monitor social media without using tools that combine all kinds of media platforms into one dashboard. These enable you to categorise channels in a structured and efficient way, so you do not have to visit each platform separately.

SWAPPING

Desk research can get expensive if you have to buy all the books, papers and magazines yourself. Organising literature swaps, where you exchange sources with your colleagues or fellow students, helps you in spreading the costs without losing out on information.

SCAN PLAN

To get started with field and desk research it helps to create a scan plan. This is an overview of field research and desk research activities you plan to execute. By making a scan plan you can create focus in your scanning process and work in a more structured way. You can make an individual plan or a team plan, you can make a plan for one day to a month to even a whole year.

> "It's key to become disciplined in using many different sources. I block a couple of days each month to read and to visit at least two exhibitions."
>
> Laura Wolfs - Senior Research Consultant at Point Blank International

The main question to be answered in your scan plan is: where are you going to find signs of change? Make a plan that includes several field research and desk research activities and specify what you are going to visit, click, watch, read or listen. You can write your plan down on paper and stick it on a wall or you can make a digital version and add all activities to an online calendar. The main thing is that you decide on how to start your spotting process and to help you in not only making a plan but also make this plan become reality.

FIELD RESEARCH

- » Interviews
- » Areas
- » Locations
- » Streets
- » Flyers hunts
- » Exhibitions
- » Events
- » Festivals
- » Trade shows

DESK RESEARCH

- » Books
- » News media
- » Magazines
- » Scientific journals
- » TV
- » Movies and series
- » Documentaries
- » TED Talks
- » Blogs and vlogs
- » Crowdfunding platforms
- » Figures and stats
- » Trend platforms
- » Social media
- » Podcasts

QUESTION ···

Can you create your own scan plan?
Make a first attempt at creating a scan plan and decide on it being
a personal plan or a team plan and for which period of time you are
making it.

Then add relevant activities divided into field and desk research and
specify what you are going to do. So not just add 'visiting an exhibition'
but also which one you are visiting and when you are going.

Discuss your scan plan with a colleague, friend or
fellow student to get more input on activities to add.

···

Keep track of everything you have done and take pictures of you executing field and desk research.
At a later stage this can be useful in communicating to a client or audience how you gathered your trend
information and provide insight into your ways of working. It makes your trend story more convincing
and validates your process and findings.

NETWORK SPOTTING
Although it is best to do most of your spotting activities alone for full immersion, it certainly helps
when more people are scanning at the same time and you can combine forces. The more eyes
watching, the more information and it also helps in assuring that various angles come into play and
a diversity of sources are consulted. The network approach has always been quite common in trend
research. In this approach of trendspotting you can divide a network into two categories: a network of
experts and frontrunners and a network of trend spotters. Take a closer look at both types of networks
and find out how to create and structure these yourself.

Network of experts and frontrunners
Spotting trends is easier when you know who the frontrunners are and go where the innovators are.
It is often hard for the general public to imagine what the future might look like and what the impact of
innovations can be on their future daily lives. Therefore trend researchers investigate what inventors,
experts and frontrunners have to say. To monitor change it is useful to create a network of experts and
frontrunners to tap into and pick their brains.

"We did a project about the future of fandom in which we collaborated with experts, like a psychologist who studied sport fans and their drivers. We also researched the future of stadiums, the future of media and the future of identity and interviewed people who were working on related projects or were experts in these domains."

Sam Shaw - Head of Insight at Canvas8

Frontrunners can be individual people, collectives or organisations and brands. They can be visionaries, nerds, academics, designers, artists, entrepreneurs or experts. You can trace these frontrunners by doing field research at the earlier mentioned locations, from the streets to trade shows. You can also locate them via your desk research because they are mentioned in books, articles and blogs or write these themselves. There is a fine line between what it means to be a frontrunner or to be an expert. Most experts can tell you a lot about the history and the status quo of their domain of expertise, whether fashion, food or health. Frontrunners within a specific domain can be experts too, but do not necessarily have to be an authority on a topic. They have a certain vision on where they would like society or a domain to move to, they challenge the status-quo and can tell you about their preferred future. When meeting these frontrunners and experts during your field research walk up to them and ask them about their projects and interests, why they are so involved in it and what their future view is on their subject of interest. Finding out what experts think and what drives and motivates frontrunners is essential input for trend research.

"We conduct interviews with topic experts related to the scope of a trend research project. These can be one-on-one interviews or panel discussions."

Claudia Lieshout - Creative Director Lifestyle Trends at Philips Design

You might feel that you do not know these type of people, but you probably know more of them than you think. Ever heard of the idea of six degrees of separation? In an interconnected world human networks are extremely close linked and you are only six or fewer personal connections away from any other human on the planet. So start mapping your own network, because to tap into these sources you have to be aware of them first.

» Who do you know personally?
Do you know everything about your family and friends? About your uncle and his circle of friends or about the network of your best friend's mother? More distant members in your social circles like colleagues, teachers, sports team members or classmates can also point you into interesting directions. Make an overview of people you know personally who have a certain kind of expertise or are working on anything innovative.

» Who have you heard of?
Then start mapping the people outside of your personal network. Who did you recently see speaking at an event and inspired you? Have you read an interview of someone in a magazine or a blog that you found interesting? Research these persons by using field research and desk research techniques and integrate them into your network overview.

To add even more people in your network, crowd source your network and use online social platforms and your offline personal network to scout frontrunners. Put out a request for finding a specific frontrunner or expert. Sites used for professional networking are handy to use for search queries or to have a quick overview on someone's CV and biography. Add anyone you have spoken to during field research and develop your own online or offline rolodex.

QUESTION ··

How to find an expert in ...?

To practice becoming more aware of your connections try to think of various search queries you can set yourself. For example: find three people who can inspire leisure marketers about where the leisure domain is heading the next couple of years.

Where would you start? Who do you know already? Who do you know who might know relevant people? Should these be only people from the leisure domain or can they also be experts or innovators from other domains?

Discuss your thoughts with a colleague or fellow student to get inspiration on different ways to tackle this search query.

··

» Maintain your network

Having a list with people's names on it does not yet create a valuable network. You will have to put effort in your network, invest in the relationships and contribute a lot yourself as well. An important aspect of networking is what you bring to the table and how this can help the others in your network to move forward. Can you connect them to relevant people in your network or can you mention them in your trend reports so they will get more coverage? Sometimes you will give more than you receive and sometimes you will get back more than you give, but networking is not about keeping score.

> *"Create a professional network and maintain it. Through conversations, meetings, coffee dates and social media posts you can feed your network with information. If you do not feed your network they will not feed you."*
>
> Zuzanna Skalska - Founding Partner of 360Inspiration

Two trend agencies that have created a network of experts and innovators share their connected approach and how they integrated this into their daily work.

A NETWORK OF SPARKS
Pernille Kok-Jensen - Connectivity Director at MARE

"Sparks is MARE's international network of people who can all be classified as experts, pioneers and trend makers in their specialist area. I'm a generalist and know a little bit about a lot, therefore I have to find people who know a lot about specific things. Having a highly curated network of visionaries on standby is an amazing way to create depth to my own generic trend hunches.

I started building the network with people who inspire me personally. I also took into account the client portfolio of MARE and the industries they cover like telecom, finance, food and public communication. I added Sparks to the network from these respective areas. Sparks are our walking talking trend encyclopaedia in flesh and blood and an important source of trend information. They are passionate and driven people who are eager to share their ideas and visions with you.

We collaborate with Sparks in various ways: online, during live workshops and in the form of trend reports. The Sparks network is a facilitator in connecting our clients with visionaries. We involve the Sparks into sometimes very complex client's issues. We once invited a creative director in the fashion industry to solve a problem for a telecom client's challenge. The fashion Spark had been struggling with the exact same innovation challenge within his industry and his vision could be transferred to a completely different industry. That's where the magic happens!"

A COMMUNITY CONNECTION TEAM
Hannah Lincoln - Culture Research Manager at China Youthology

"Our community team is constantly recruiting thought leaders within the domain of youth culture. These are youngsters who are insiders and part of a specific cultural scene. Maintaining this community is not about paying members incentives. Our team really bonds with them, follows them on social media and meets them at events. This type of recruiting is about keeping connections warm, recycling energy between each other and respecting each other. It is a two-way street because they also get resources from us, we give them a platform and connect them with brands.

This type of network is the lifeblood of what we do at China Youthology. We cannot do trend research by talking to people who are just meeting some demographic criteria like a specific age or gender, we need to find the influencers and innovators."

Network of trends spotters

Next to a network of experts and innovators, you can also create a network to help you spot more signs of change. Since quantity is crucial in the first step of scanning, it can be worthwhile to collaborate with other trend spotters who also like to spot the next and the new. These tend to be generalists rather than experts and the focus is on their spotting skills rather than specific domain knowledge. When creating a team or network of spotters think of the characteristics these spotters should have as stated in chapter one. Can you find people who, at least partly, have the personality traits of a trend researcher? To take a structured approach, you can think of ways of creating a formal spotters network which can be divided in several ways, for instance:

» Local spotters, who are located in various regions within a country or all over the world. They have their ear to local ground and spot things you cannot because you are living on the other side of the country or the world.
» Target group spotters, people who belong to a specific target group you are interested in and which you are not part of yourself.
» Sector related spotters, people who are involved in a certain domain and are more in the know and have easier access to domain involved sources than you have.

> "We have a worldwide network of trend spotters who can assist us in doing trend research. If, for instance, the scope of a project is the Russian market and consumers then we would always collaborate with a local Russian trend expert who understands the culture and has access to Russian sources."
>
> Claudia Lieshout - Creative Director Lifestyle Trends at Philips Design

Your task as the main node in this spotters network is to brief these spotters, stimulate them to spot, collect all information and add it to your own spotting materials. While the spotter's task is to spot, yours as the researcher is to layer all findings, select the most relevant signs from the pile and archive them in a way that they are ready for the analysis phase. An important and time-consuming task is to keep spotters motivated to submit spots. Money might seem as the perfect incentive for a spotter but many trendspotting networks use different types of rewards. Gamification elements come into play and spotters can earn points which are redeemable for certain privileges like access to events and seminars or vouchers to buy innovative products. Being elected as trend spotter of the month or getting featured in a trend publication can also be a reward.

Two trend agencies which have created a network of trend spotters share their approach and how they integrate this into in their daily work.

TW:IN SPOTTERS
Victoria Foster - Head of tw:in at Trendwatching

"We have a worldwide network of 3000 trend spotters called tw:in. It is made up of forward-thinking individuals from Moscow to Manila and Beijing to Boston, who share an insatiable curiosity to uncover the most compelling, exciting and interesting innovations that highlight the direction of trends around the globe. Via our online platform we send out monthly trend challenges and spotters submit all kinds of signs of innovation related to a challenge. Our content team filters and analyses these. They compare the spots to see if they match any of our trends in our framework or if new expectations are forming.

For example, a while ago we had the insight that a trend was emerging about subversive brands. These brands were being bold in their marketing and taking an impactful stance against a competitor. This trend originated from an innovation one of our Hong Kong spotters had sent us about a local craft ale bar where you could get free entrance by bringing a cheap can of lager which the bartenders would then crush to make a statement. We then asked our network of Spotters if they had seen anything new happening in a similar line in their country or culture. We wanted to know more about the next evolution on how this trend was changing around the world. When an entry peaks our interest a Spotter can earn points and redeem those for things like books or Amazon vouchers.

Our Spotters are our sounding board in researching trends. Although we have offices around the globe we can still get stuck in our own bubble and lose perspective on what's going in the world. The key thing what makes our trend content so much richer is our global view we create via our network of Spotters."

The tw:in network.

A NETWORK OF COOLHUNTERS
Carl Rohde - Culture Sociologist and founder of Science of the Time

"I feel you need to be able to substantiate and justify everything you are saying about trends for which I feel it is important not to observe on your own. Science of the Time is a futures research consultancy agency with a virtual network of coolhunters worldwide. I've trained and collaborated with thousands of, what we call, coolhunters and this makes me see the world through their eyes and not only my own.

Having access to a worldwide network of spotters is crucial to orientate yourself in a broader way than just your personal perspective. Our method is called coolhunting and we have trained students at dozens of universities around the world to find signs of what they perceive as cool. Cool in our vision means it has to be an attractive and inspiring manifestation of change with future growth potential.

I have access to thousands of eyeballs scanning the world for these cool seeds of the new and blogging about it on our Science of the Time platform. We have created a virtual workspace that is open 24/7, where coolhunters can upload their findings and share them with the Science of the Time community to get feedback. This interactive feedback element is crucial in our networked way of working, because the more you put in it, the more you get out of it. It is important to compare what you have spotted with others and an online platform is great for just that."

STEP 2: SELECT

You have collected loads of trend spots and might now feel overloaded with information. This means it is time to take the next step in the scanning phase: select. When you glance over your spots for a second time you probably feel some of them are popping out more than others. Selecting is about cherry picking the most relevant signs and making a first rough cut. You can do this by asking yourself questions about every single trend spot. Crucial in this step is that you dare to make choices and delete, discard and throw away some of your findings.

> "Today's news is tomorrow's chip shop paper, so when spotting signals I always ask myself:
> if I would look back at this sign in six months, would it still be relevant or would it be a sloppy
> signal that faded away?"
>
> Sam Shaw - Head of Insight at Canvas8

How do you decide what is most relevant? To be able to select the most interesting spots you can use a checklist of questions to assess the relevancy of everything you have spotted. Seasoned trend researchers have these questions in the back of their minds while spotting and every time they spot something interesting they automatically check the relevancy of it.

> "Already while reading and watching I can find patterns, I compare it to other things I have seen
> or read before and look for repetition."
>
> Juan Pablo Zapata Barros - Freelance Trend Researcher

To experiment with selecting, first spot many signs of change, pile them up and then start the selection process. Check every trend spot one by one and ask yourself critical questions, like the ones proposed in the following checklist.

SELECT CHECKLIST

- » Is your spot innovative?
- » Is your spot inspiring?
- » Is your spot clear?
- » Is your spot reliable?
- » Is your spot an anomaly?
- » Is your spot creating impact?

» **Is your spot innovative?**
How new and up to date is your signal? Maybe you personally think that a lot of your signals and observations are new but are they new to others too? Is your spot a really wild sign of change or is it a more established kind of sign? You can check this by asking around and checking with others if they have heard about the sign. Or you can research the sign some more online, see how many hits you get

89

and how recent these are. Getting a feel for newness is something you can train by spotting often and creating a benchmark to compare your findings with.

> *"New is a relative term, it depends on the audience and on yourself if something is new or not. There is always someone for whom the signal you found is not new, while for others the same signal can feel radically new."*
>
> Cornelia Daheim - Principal of Future Impact

» **Is your spot inspiring?**
How inspiring is the manifestation you spotted? Start by asking yourself why you find it inspiring, what aspects make this sign stand out to you? Then ask yourself why someone else could also find it inspiring or not. If you tell others about it, how do they react? Does it create a specific effect with people and how intense is the reaction?

» **Is your spot clear?**
How understandable is your spotted signal? Is it easy to communicate in one or two sentences or with one image? Some spots can be hard to explain, for instance a new business model or a new body of thought. Some signs can be ambiguous and might be understood the wrong way. That does not make the sign irrelevant but harder to use, because it needs a lot of explaining. Maybe you can find another signal in the same category which is easier to understand?

» **Is your spot reliable?**
How trustworthy is your spot? Did you double check the main source? Try to work as a journalist and validate your sources. Be aware that news media are not as objective as you might think and individual's blogs or vlogs can also hold non-factual information or hoaxes. Especially when it comes to numbers it is best to fact-check as thoroughly as you can.

> *"I use information from multiple resources and check if they are saying the same thing in a meaningful way or if they are just copying one another. When it comes to numbers, I always check if they came from reliable sources and if they clarify and support my trends.*
>
> Niels van der Burg - Global Category Insights Manager at Asics

» **Is your spot an anomaly?**
Have you encountered this spot or similar ones frequently during desk and field research? Or do you just have one or two sources that show this sign of change? If so, it might be a weak signal, and you should monitor it more to decide if it is an anomaly, an odd exception or an emerging sign of change. This does not mean that the sign is irrelevant but that it might be too early to use it in your trend analysis and share it with an audience.

» **Is your spot creating impact?**
What kind of impact could your sign generate in the world? Think about how your spotted manifestation might influence the future quality of life of people. What kind of potential does this seed of change hold for the future? A new kind of hairstyle is probably less impactful than a new way of thinking or a disruptive new technology. It helps to ask yourself what would happen if a spot would become part of our daily lives.

IT IS IMPORTANT TO SEE WHAT IS INVISIBLE TO OTHERS.

"Innovation for me is not just about shiny technological features, it is about considering the social and environmental impact too. What's the purpose of a new technology, is it creating something meaningful, is it adding value to people's lives and to our planet?"
Valeria Ossio - Service & Strategic Designer at Mandalah

The step of selecting requires you to be critical and to be as objective as possible. Remember that the relevancy of your sign is determined by all of the questions and not just one. Answering these questions might mean you have to research your spots some more. This step shows a fine line between the scanning and analysing phases because you are already making a first rough analysis of each sign. When in doubt about holding on to a sign or deleting it, do some quick extra research. Discuss the topic with colleagues, fellow students, friends or experts or search online for more information. Although working with a checklist of questions seems quite rational and analytic, intuition is also at play when selecting the most relevant manifestations. To answer the questions there are often no facts and figures to help you out in deciding if a spot is new and understandable enough.

"Intuition is not the sixth sense, it is the first sense! You should be aware that there is a difference between knowledge and knowing. While knowledge is about building a repository of data, knowing is inner, intuitive and surpasses all the books."
Kristina Dryža - Global Director of Trends and Futures at House of Brand Group

As mentioned earlier, for experienced researchers making a first rough selection of their spots comes almost natural. When your training increases you will be able to do the same because you have created a frame of reference to compare spots with.

"You get totally different results when you compare someone who just starts out with trend scanning and someone who has done it for five years. When you have practiced a lot, you get a better understanding of systems in the world and the underlying drivers of change."
Cornelia Daheim - Principal of Future Impact

STEP 3: DOCUMENT

Now you have a smaller pile of trend spots left, what do you do with these? The last step in the scanning process is to dive into the selected trend spots and get to the nitty gritty of them. You really need to know every selected sign back to front and archive all your findings in a way you can retrieve everything easily again. After making the first rough cut in your signals and manifestations you can start doing some more research on them. This way you really get to know the ins and outs of every spot and know how to file them better in your database. Your audience or clients can ask you any kind of question about your signs if you use them in presentations or reports. You should be prepared and be able to answer these. For this you will need to make an effort in knowing everything about every spot.

> *"When I started out as a trend researcher I made mistakes like pronouncing a product name the wrong way during a live trend presentation. That would never happen now, because I research better and know every detail about my trend examples."*
>
> Cécile Cremer - Founder of Trends & Innovation Agency Wandering the Future and former Fontys ILS student

DESCRIPTION

To guide you in getting to know your spots you can use a checklist of features to research. This will help you to make the description of every trend spot more complete and create a full picture of every manifestation of change. For every selected sign you can make short descriptions of the signs features and attributes. This will help you to be prepared for any questions if you would use this sign as an example in a presentation or report.

DESCRIPTION CHECKLIST

- » What is it?
- » How does it work?
- » What is the launch date?
- » Who is the inventor?
- » Where is it spotted?
- » Which domain is it linked to?
- » How does it relate to quality of life?
- » What is the main source of reference?

» **What is it?**
Describe the core of the trend spot. What is it, is it a book, an event, a product, a style, a service, a model, a theory? And what is the spot about? Try to describe the core of the spot in just a couple of sentences.

» **How does it work?**
Describe the idea behind your spot and the process behind it. Which advantages does this spot offer to people and what are the costs, whether in money, time or effort?

» **What is the launch date?**
When was this spot first launched, created, presented or noticed? Can you find anything related to this about your spot? It will help you to define the newness of it.

» **Who is the inventor?**
Who is the person or company behind this spot? Who or what created it? Try to find out about the makers and producers motivations for doing so too. This can be crucial in the analysis phase.

» **Where is it spotted?**
What is the location where this spot is currently most active and observable? Is it seen in a specific country, region, culture or within a certain target group?

» **Which domain is it linked to?**
In which domain does your spot fall? Is it linked to categories like health, leisure, food or any other sectors? This can be helpful to tag your spots when archiving them and also to notice if innovations are spotted more in a certain domain than in others.

» **How does it relate to quality of life?**
Which aspects of quality of life (Felce, 1995) does your spot link to? Does it relate to physical wellbeing, material wellbeing, social wellbeing, emotional wellbeing, development and activity or a certain combination of those?

» **What is the main source of reference?**
Where did you find the most relevant background information about the sign? This might be on a corporate web page, in a background article or via an interview you did yourself. A main source is helpful to mention in a presentation or report so others can check it too.

FILING

The last action to take in documenting is filing these descriptions because relying on your memory is not advisable when archiving trend spots. Maybe at the beginning you might feel you will be able to remember all your spots, but when you are spotting for months on end this will not be feasible anymore. Archiving your information is crucial in trend research and to finish the scanning phase you should find a way to file your findings somewhere external so you can take a trip down to memory lane anytime you like. You might not use every trend spot right away but they can be useful at another time, for example when a project asks for it and you want to retrieve it at a specific desired moment.

Filing criteria
To create your own way of documenting and to decide on how to archive your trend spots the following can be considered:

» Amount of users
Are you the only one using the archiving system or are others too? If you are the only one using it, you can personalise it in a way you like it. But when others, such as colleagues or clients, should be able to use it too then you should think of a system that is easy for anyone to use. You could create a system together with the other users and make an inventory of which filing criteria matter most to them.

» Visual or text driven
Do you want a visual focussed archiving system, a text driven one or a combination of both? Some people can remember and search things easier with visual clues, others with text. Decide which works for you.

» Analogue or digital
Do you prefer an analogue or digital way of filing information? Each has its strengths and weaknesses. When you like to hold on to something physically, create an overview on a wall or leave through pages, then analogue is the way to go. If you like to be able to use a search tool and take your archive anywhere you want, then digital is the way to go. A combination of both analogue and digital systems is possible too.

» System of tagging
Randomly saving information in a system is not recommended because information will pile causing a feeling of information overload instead of being in control of your spots. Creating a category structure upfront will help you to find stored spots quicker within an archiving system, whether it is labelling your paper folders to tagging smart in digital tools. Think of categories for tagging, such as industry sectors, mentality groups, regions or anything else that is relevant to you.

Filing examples
Trend researchers each have their own personal preferences in setting up a trend database. Take a look at some of these filing systems to help you in finding your personal way of archiving your selected spots.

» Notebooks
You can carry a notebook and file things that stand out to you by writing them down, drawing them or cutting and pasting them in. You can use a dummy and turn it into your personalised trend scrapbook. This type of filing is suitable when you use it as a personal archive but it is harder to share with a group of people.

> *"I like to use A6 paper notebooks which fit into my pants' back pockets."*
> Rodrigo dos Reis - Consumer Trends Specialist at Zeitgeist

» Dossiers
You can file your trend spots in an analogue way by creating trend dossiers, where you file cut outs of articles, visuals and your own personal paper notes. This type of archiving can be used within a team too, but is not accessible from other locations easily.

"I always mark words, sentences and quotes in newspapers, cut them out and archive them. I have rows of dossiers in my study divided into specific sectors and mentality groups."

Carl Rohde - Culture Sociologist and founder of Science of the Time

» Evidence wall

It can be handy to collect all trend spots on a wall to create a visual overview. To observe all information within a confined space helps you to select and cluster. You can create a wall at home or at the office, where it also serves as a reminder for others to stick their spots on the wall. The disadvantages being that is has no search function and you cannot take it with you easily.

"It was really great to be able to put down everything I spotted on a surface. Using a wall creates an overview and I like that you can really hold your spots and move things around."

Fleur Stiels - Concept Developer at Dutch Rose Media and former Fontys ILS student

» Digital folders

You can create digital folders on your personal computer or in the cloud to make them even more accessible, also to others. This way of filing requires you to think of ways of naming your files and folders in a logical way.

"When I read interesting things I copy-paste these texts into a word file on my laptop, because next to having a digital version, I like to be able to print it out and have something tangible in my hands."

Niels van der Burg - Global Category Insights Manager at Asics

"I take a lot of photos and videos. I place them in project based folders on my laptop."

Rodrigo dos Reis - Consumer Trends Specialist at Zeitgeist

» Company databases

Some organisations have created their own databases that allow employees to access it anytime to stay updated on anything added and add their own spots too.

» External platforms

If you do not have the budget to buy a personalised database system you can use an online external platform which can be subscription based or free of charge. You can assign people to access this platform or keep your folders private. Most of these systems are accessible from any device.

"We have a subscription to Evernote and create folders with a chronological numbered system where we archive all signals. We tag them in categories like feminism or sports."

Hannah Lincoln - Culture Research Manager at China Youthology

To find out what works best for you, experiment with the different kinds of filing systems and combinations. Remember that the aim of filing is to retrieve information as quickly as you can, do not get caught in a web of complex archives.

≡ SUMMARY

» Scanning is the crucial first phase in trend research: no signals, no evidence.

» Scanning is about spotting across domains, lifestyles and regions.

» Scanning can be done in a structured three step way: spot, select and document.

SPOT

» Spotting is about finding as many manifestations of change as you can.

» Spotting activities can be divided into doing field research and desk research.

» Spotting can be done alone or in collaboration with a network of experts or spotters.

SELECT

» After spotting you will have to make a first rough selection of the most relevant spots.

» To decide on the relevancy you can ask yourself critical questions about each spot.

DOCUMENT

» Documenting requires you to enrich and describe the features of every selected spot.

» Documenting is also about creating a suitable archiving system to file every spot.

= WANT TO KNOW MORE?

Eager to learn more about the scanning phase of trend research? Here you can find some suggestions for further reading, watching and clicking. This is only a selection of a vast array of sources. You can find more information at www. howtoresearchtrends.com.

UNLOCK YOUR SENSES

These sources can help you to trigger your senses:

» How to be an Explorer of the World, a book by Keri Smith
» The Wander Society, a book by Keri Smith
» How to Think Like Leonardo da Vinci, a book by Michael J. Gelb
» The Modern Day Spotter's Guide, a book by Richard Horne
» The Art of Looking Sideways, a book by Alan Fletcher
» On Looking, a book by Alexandra Horowitz
» Be inspired by videos about people who are masters in using one or more senses like Sissel Tolaas's videos on smell which you can find on channels like YouTube.

IMPROVE YOUR SEARCH SKILLS

Train your web search skills by using tutorials, for instance 'power searching' with Google. Other useful tools by Google are:

» Google Alerts: lets you monitor specific keywords and sends a notification when they are used online.
» Google News: a site that aggregates headlines from news sources worldwide.
» Google Trends: a tool that shows how often specific keywords, subjects and phrases have been queried over a specific period of time.

FASTER, FASTER!

To help you read texts faster you can use online applications like Spreeder, Spritz or 7speedreading.

LET'S MEET ··

To find interesting events around the world use tools like Meetup or Facebook events, which facilitate offline group meetings unified by a common interest. You can also start your own themed Meet-up or Facebook event.

HOTSPOTS ···

City blogs and city magazines can point you in the direction of interesting places to visit or events to attend. From worldwide ones like Time Out to local ones like A-Mag showcasing the latest in the city of Amsterdam.

TRADE SHOWS ···

To search for a trade show to visit you can use calendars on sites like Expo Database or The Tradeshow Network. You can easily search for trade shows by date, region or domain.

BECOME A BOOKWORM ···

To get recommendations for books to read you can use diverse resources:

» tips by trend professionals, like the library lists of Science of the Time
» tips by a community of readers, like the reviews on sites like Goodreads
» tips by journalists, like the book sections in (inter)national news media like The New York Times or The Guardian.

OTHER DESK RESEARCH SOURCES ···

» Online news media, like The Huffington Post or Medium
» Lifestyle oriented magazines, like Vogue or ID
» Domain focused magazines, like Wired or The Economist.
» Science fiction movies and series, like Star Trek, which show future oriented technology and its impact on the lives of the people on the star ships
» Crowdsourcing platforms, like Kickstarter
» Statistics institutions, like Eurostat
» Commercial market analysis agencies, like Euromonitor or GfK.

TOOLS TO SAVE AND ARCHIVE ···

These are some tools to archive your spots. These are continuously replaced by newer and better ones, so always be on the look-out for new tools.

- » Feedly, an RSS feed application that aggregates news and allows you to organise, read and share it with others.
- » Pocket, a tool to save articles and videos to read later.
- » Evernote, note-taking and archiving tool for collecting information, keeping it all organised and collaborating with others. There is a free version or a subscription based fee for unlimited storage.
- » Social media management tools, like Hootsuite and Tweetdeck, to help you organise social media feeds and categorise these easily.
- » Flipboard, an application that aggregates content from social media, news feeds, photo sharing sites and other websites and presents it in magazine format.

#4

ANALYSE

CONNECTING THE DOTS

One manifestation of change is not yet
a trend. In this chapter you will learn
how to analyse your findings and move
from trend spots to underlying insights.
You will also learn to master the art of
naming trends and visualising them in
an inspiring way.

+ TOPICS

+ INTRO

Detecting manifestations of change is one task of a trend researcher. The next is to give meaning to these observations and try to understand what they reveal about the future. Analysing your trend spots is like piecing a puzzle to connect the dots and find patterns of change. You need to find these underlying values to be able to apply trends because these form the basis to innovate on.

"Rattling off a load of facts without any context is not useful to your audience. What do these mean? That's where trend researchers can add value."

Kelly McKnight - Head of Culture & Trends at Join the Dots

In this chapter you will move from trend spots to underlying trend insights. You will combine your spots into meaningful trend clusters, validate and back these with more evidence to create coherent trend storylines. And last but not least, you will label your trend clusters with catchy names and inspiring visuals that represent the core of each trend. In this way you will create your first trend overview, which can be used as a springboard for the apply phase.

PIECING THE PUZZLE

Analysis is about comparing your spots and noticing differences and similarities that point towards certain patterns. The aim of a trend analysis is to have a better understanding of what is going on in society right now and how this might impact the future. During analysis you establish links and find relationships between manifestations that at first sight might feel unrelated.

> *"To me analysing trends is about deleting and adding data, combining information and looking for an overlap."*
>
> Niels van der Burg - Global Category Insights Manager at Asics

Analysis is about finding meaning that goes beyond the surface of your trend spots, so go beyond features and finishes to find the deeper meaning. For trend researchers a new technology or style per se is not the most interesting, but the meaning behind it is. Key in analysis is that you ask 'why' all the time. Why do people want to use, buy or show a certain innovation? What does it add to their quality of life? Which values does it link to and which needs does it meet?

> *"It is like the work of an archaeologist. You find a small piece, like one bone, and then you have to imagine what the whole dinosaur would have looked like. The same goes for trend analysis."*
>
> Zuzanna Skalska - Founding Partner of 360Inspiration

Analysing your trend findings is a subjective activity as is all analysis of information gathered via a qualitative approach. When analysing trends you have to get comfortable with ambiguity. To lower subjectivity and to challenge your own thoughts it is key to discuss your analysis with others. Make it a team activity, have conversations and debates to question your own interpretations. This cross-reference of findings can be done in all kinds of ways, from just an informal chat with friends and family to structured ways of exchanging views with fellow team members, experts or your clients.

> *"Analysing really is a collaborative effort. At our agency we get together once in a while to share and analyse findings. I also analyse together with my students in coolhunting and their lecturers. And last but not least, I also analyse my findings with my commercial clients via brainstorming sessions."*
>
> Carl Rohde - Culture Sociologist and founder of Science of the Time

ANALYSE STEPS

Most people who analyse trends for the first time feel a bit uneasy about where to start. It helps to set up your analysis in a structured manner to stay in control of the process. This also makes it easier to explain to others what you have been doing and communicate about your analysis in a transparent way. To help you get started, the analysing process is divided into three steps: Cluster, Validate and Label. On the following pages you will dive into every step and understand how to use these steps to create your first trend overview.

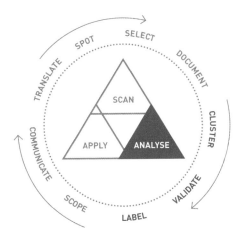

STEP 1: CLUSTER

Analysing starts with using the output of the scan phase and clustering your trend spots. When you look at these spots, which of these seem to address the same underlying values and needs? Can you find common themes running through them? In this section you will be updated on how to cluster your trend spots.

STEP 2: VALIDATE

Dig deeper into your trend clusters and develop a coherent, thorough and inspiring trend storyline per cluster. You zoom in on every cluster and try to underpin why this specific change is happening right now, how it has emerged and how it might evolve. This segment will show you which questions to ask yourself to drill down your trend clusters.

STEP 3: LABEL

During this final step of the analysis phase you will capture each detailed, validated trend in a single name with accompanying key visuals that represent the trend in an inspiring and meaningful way. In this part you will read about various ways of labelling and visualising trends.

STEP 1: CLUSTER

The first step in the analysis phase is to start clustering your manifestations of change, because one observation is just that, a single observation. You will have to find out if your observations are signs of something bigger happening. Clustering is about moving from signs to meaning. You will need to sift through your collection of trend spots and find the underlying values and needs related to each spot. Clustering is about combining an analytic mind-set with a creative one. This goes beyond just keeping score and adding up types of new products or behaviours you have seen. You must be able to see patterns in unexpected ways that might seem unrelated at first. Finding patterns and relationships between trend manifestations is a continuous process. Professional trend researchers often analyse while scanning. They constantly compare a manifestation to others they have spotted before in the back of their mind.

The starting point of clustering is the collection of trend spots in your trend database. These spots can have different formats, from digital information to physical objects. When you want to identify patterns it is helpful to create an overview of what you have spotted so you can hover above it, like a helicopter.

> *"You have to orbit and see everything from above. You have to be able to change your perspective on subjects. When you feel that something is not fitting, you can move things around and find a pattern."*
>
> Zuzanna Skalska - Founding Partner of 360Inspiration

You can create digital or analogue displays of your information on walls, tables, windows, movable screens or via online tools for mind mapping. When doing it in an analogue way it is best to have a designated space for your overview where it can stay for a longer period of time. This way you can review and reflect on your collection and add or delete signs throughout the clustering process.

> *"I approach analysing as a design process. I need to see everything at a glance together so I print out all the things I found and put them on a wall. This makes it easier for me and others to see connections."*
>
> Valeria Ossio - Service & Strategic Designer at Mandalah

When you have found a way to display your collection of signs it is time to start clustering. The aim of clustering is to find relations between spots that point to shifts in people's values and needs. Related spots form a trend cluster which you can validate (or not) in the next step of the analysis phase. The process of clustering is one of observing, combining, identifying, discussing and deleting. Preferably you would do clustering in a group to not get stuck in your own point of view and perspective. This way everybody can add their spots to the display, explain and pitch these to others, discuss and exchange views.

> *"Check all the information you have gathered together as a team and look for similarities. Be flexible and don't pin yourself down to a fixed amount of themes. You might start with fifty signals and go through it again and again to define the themes."*
>
> Sam Shaw - Head of Insight at Canvas8

It can help to structure this process in a few stages. Consider the proposed steps in the cluster checklist below:

CLUSTER CHECKLIST

» Prepare the session
» Share spots
» Discuss and combine
» Add values
» Assign keywords
» Reflect and adjust

» Prepare the session

When working in a team, reserve a time slot in every participant's agenda. Assign a specific space for the cluster session where you can easily move furniture around and attach things on a surface. Preferably this space is quiet, light and airy and blocks out external stimuli. Make sure there is enough food and drink for the duration of the session. When working in a team you can assign participants with homework, for example 'bring prints of ten signs to the session'.

» Share spots

When everybody is in the room, start out with collecting everyone's spots and create a display, whether digital or analogue. Look at all the spots individually and write down first thoughts on paper, post-its or any way you prefer.

» Discuss and combine

Discuss the signs amongst each other and try to find connections between them. Are there more of the same kind of observations? What are the similarities and what are the differences? Cluster the signs based roughly on what they are telling you beyond their surface. This means thinking on a more abstract level than just combining signs into features like 'computer games' or 'sweaters'. Can you find common denominators? Did you see the same kind of spots happening in different sectors or regions? Move the spots around to get inspiration from unexpected combinations. Take another look at the left-over signals, are there more signals that belong to the just created trend clusters?

» Add values

Discuss the clusters and signs related to them to explore the underlying values and needs. Remember that the manifestations are representations of emerging values and needs people feel are worth pursuing. It can help to have a cheat sheet with the values of Rokeach (or any other value related model you are familiar with) printed on it to remind you of the type of words you can use to describe the underlying feelings. In the end it is not about the model but about finding trend insights from other people's perspective. You can use a qualitative research technique called laddering to get to the core values and needs behind a manifestation. Learn more about this in the next text box.

TOOL: **LADDERING**

Normally this technique is used during interviews in market research with a specific target group for the purposes of uncovering the underlying emotions, consequences and personal values that drive people's choices. In trend research you can use it too by applying it in clustering sessions or also to question your own way of reasoning. The technique is to ask 'why?' as many times as needed to get to the core motivator behind a manifestation. This way of reasoning is also known as the means-end chain, which is a value chain linking a product or service attribute (the manifestation) from its functional consequence, to the psychosocial or emotional consequence and finally to the underlying personal values. Discuss with others to get from a feature of a manifestation to a consequence to a value.

> "Name the clusters in a way that transcends the domain or category features. So do not call a cluster 'digital media' but try to use words that link to what digital media mean to people."

Valeria Ossio - Service & Strategic Designer at Mandalah

Example of how asking why (and other questions) can work:

Why do you feel this [insert trend spot] is a key signal?
It just stands out to me

Why does it stand out to you?
Because the way it is designed really is different

Why do you feel the design is different?
It has different colour scheme than these normally have

In what exactly does this one differ?
Normally it would be more toned down but this one is quite bright

What does this brightness imply, how does that make you feel?
It makes me feel light hearted and happy

And so on....

Trend #4 Roots & Wings

ROOTS & WINGS

#RECOGNITION
#SOCIALITY
#APPRECIATION
#EXCITE

Jeff Wall
De Pont

Anish Kapoor
De Pont

» **Assign keywords**
Describe your clusters in a couple of keywords or a sentence. Use words that indicate what change in feelings, attitudes and values lie behind this cluster. Try to find consensus about the words assigned to the clusters, but also remember this is the first attempt to create them and you can still change them later.

» **Reflect and adjust**
Do not over-haste the clustering process. It is important to take some time and space to reflect on it. During sessions you can take a break and go for a walk to clear your mind. After the first session, let it all sink in and reflect on it the next day or the next week.

CLUSTERING AT MARE
Pernille Kok-Jensen - Connectivity Director at MARE

"I can illustrate our way of clustering by using an older example. A couple of years ago at the Design Academy graduation show, we saw a beautiful ceramic set of larger than life spinners. When asked, the young designer explained to us the aim was to let grown-ups freeze time and take time to play.

When walking through the streets we spotted new shops, like barber shops popping up and other shops that sell one type of item like soups or salads. You enter these shops, talk to the owners and ask them why they are opening this shop and their vision behind it. They tell us that they all focus on doing one thing really well and giving it all their attention.

We read an article about a club in Amsterdam that organised dance nights where using a camera was forbidden. They handed out stickers to clubbers to put over their cell phone camera which said: no photos, enjoy the moment. The interview had quotes in it from the event organisers stating that they wanted people to focus more on the music and the artist and taking photos creates too much distraction.

These are just three examples of the many more we have collected. But what do a spinning toy, a barber shop and a sticker for a phone camera have in common? If you would look at them at the surface, they might seem totally unrelated. But when you take a closer look at their meaning and the values they link to, then they start to make sense. Can you already see the common denominator?

We have clustered these and felt they represented an emerging mind-set that can be described by the following keywords: amazement, wonder, slow down, find balance, focus and attention. So this is where the analysis brings you to a level higher than just describing the signs for their features, as in barbershops, toys and a sticker."

The output of clustering are rough trend clusters to be researched further in the next step: validate. To record the work you have done while clustering save materials like post-its, flipcharts, take photos of walls and write down the clusters.

> "When analysing we create an overview of all relevant trend territories, we add keywords to each one and then try to see how these connect and get a stream of thought going. When we finish our analysis the flipcharts can be a bit messy and we redesign the developed trend map."
>
> Laura Wolfs - Senior Research Consultant at Point Blank International

---

CLUSTERING AT PHILIPS

Claudia Lieshout - Creative Director Lifestyle Trends at Philips Design

"To me analysis is like trend engineering or trend designing. You need to have a kind of spatial reasoning and be able to oversee your trend spots. You should not think in a one dimensional way. You need to ask yourself all sorts of questions while analysing, this should come naturally. Not everybody has that skill, it's an instinct and a gut feeling. To me it happens automatically in my head, for instance, after reading a certain article I would connect it with something I saw at an expo and understand that both are telling the same kind of story."

Researching trends is not only about observing change but also about analysing it, making connections and translating these into specific trend themes. At Philips we use a holistic perspective and look at the system as a whole. When you spread your trend information on a systemic map, you gain a better view on the most relevant touchpoints.

We organise analysis sessions where we would first create a landscape of trends in which all participants can present their information. The tools we use to cluster differ every time. Sometimes we use mind maps where we put a trend manifestation in the middle and make branches with groups of other trend examples. This way of clustering is quite organic. At other times we use grids and coordinate systems to analyse our findings, for instance value grids, category grids or timeframe grids."

CLUSTERING AT CHINA YOUTHOLOGY
Hannah Lincoln - Culture Research Manager at China Youthology

"Every quarter we analyse the signals our team and our youth insider's community have collected for the past three months. The first round of analysing is a four hour workshop together with some of the youth insiders, because they can tell us what their spotted signals mean. Sometimes one signal can be enough to point you towards a direction or a pattern, sometimes more brainpower and more signals are needed.

We often have over three hundred signals! The first hour of the workshop consists of a silent review where we take a look at as many signals as we can, while making mental or physical notes. Then we get seated in a circle and everyone shares their key notes and connects their findings with those of others. This way we start to shave off our trend sculpture.

For instance, when we find all kinds of signals related to cars or to family life it is important during analysis not to stay within these market categories, because the combination of these signals might show a shift in how youngsters perceive mobility. Working in a checkerboard way with grids can be helpful but can also be inefficient if you tend to cluster too much around markets and domains instead of the human values.

After this first round of analysis we have hunches about directions of change, probably about ten to fifteen trend clusters, and we will carve those out more clearly. We ask our youth insiders to gather more information about these directions. Finally we share and discuss these clusters with our senior team members, they bring in the long term picture and context for the clustered signals."

STEP 2: VALIDATE

The second step in the analysis phase is to see if you can validate your trend clusters. Validating your clusters is about diving into each cluster and find more information related to each trend theme. The clusters are the skeletons of each trend and now you can create a storyline by elaborating on these first findings. This means searching for more evidence to build a trend foundation, while staying critical and allowing clusters to be adjusted or deleted because your first hunch might be too far off. The output of this validation process are trend descriptions that have an inspiring narrative as well as a solid backbone enriched with sources and argumentation. Because in the end you want to deliver trend insights that inspire and inform your audience.

> "I found several signs in Mexico about Do-It-Yourself festivals that have a bottom-up approach. So I dived deeper into this matter to understand what was going on. I read interviews with festival organisers, checked blogs of visitors, searched and found more similar examples, also in other domains. I call this layering my research where I'm on a quest to create a complete trend story."
>
> Juan Pablo Zapata Barros - Freelance Trend Researcher

The most important thing to think of before you start the validation process is to decide on a trend description format. What kind of information do you need to validate if your first rough trend clusters have a reason to exist? This format is the backbone of your trend analysis and storyline. Trend professionals often describe trends using a specific structure. While the output of their trend analysis might vary, the underlying foundation of the analysis itself is often the same. It helps in this stage of the analysis to use questions as a starting point, which you try to answer to validate your trends. If you cannot answer these questions sufficiently it is possibly a sign that your trend cluster is too weak or too wild and you need to delete it or put it on hold for now.

> "Merely stating that there is a change is not enough. Ask yourself: what is changing? What was it like before and what is it like now? How does this make sense? What is the context of the trend? Then you really understand the change and the social drivers behind it."
>
> Hannah Lincoln - Culture Research Manager at China Youthology

A checklist of topics or questions can help to structure your thoughts and direct any additional research activities, so the first thing to do is to decide on these topics or questions. You can apply the suggested checklist with widely used questions and add any additional questions relevant for your specific project or organisation. The answers to these questions can be found using various sources in different formats, from texts to images.

> "We structure our analysis according to topics we would like to know about every trend, which for us are: drivers, impacts and consequences."
>
> Nadines Guhlich - Audience Research Lead at Soundcloud

VALIDATE CHECKLIST

» Why is this trend happening right now?
» What is the specific shift in values and needs?
» Who started this trend and who is spreading it?
» Which phase is the trend in?
» Where can you see this trend happening already?
» What consequences can this trend have on our future quality of life?

How to find answers to these questions will be addressed on the next pages, but before you move into that stage, consider some other relevant aspects of setting up your trend validation first. You will need to think about who is going to execute the validation work. Are you doing it on your own or will it be a team effort? If you are doing it on your own it helps to find a sparring partner during the process so you do not get stuck too much in your own train of thought.

> *"Because I mainly did research alone I went to look for a sparring partner. I collaborated with someone, who is an editor as well as a researcher and already worked on a lot of publications related to government communication. She helped me to categorise and structure my findings and write down complex matters in a simple way."*
> Rita Timmerman - Senior Research Consultant at the Dutch Ministry of General Affairs

If you are going to work together with others, you can divide the clusters amongst every team member. Everyone should apply the same format to work on each of their assigned trend clusters. You can organise a review loop, where each team member forwards their finished descriptions to other team members to give and get feedback on revisions to be made. Make sure you keep track of all the sources you use during the process of your validation research. Create a list of references and decide on the way to document these. You can use publication guidelines such as the APA-style, which is common practice in many social sciences.

When you have agreed on which format to use, you can start out with filling in the blanks. There are many ways of validating your trend clusters, of which many have already been mentioned in the earlier chapters. You can do additional desk and field research and use tools like STEEP or theories like Rogers' diffusion of innovation theory. For every question in the validation checklist you will now get some pointers on what to look for and how to look for it.

» **Why is this trend happening right now?**
Where did it emerge from into where it is now? What are the main drivers making it possible for it to emerge now? These questions all address the evolution of a trend cluster. You will need to look into the past and dig up some historical facts to understand why a certain shift is emerging at this moment in time. Trends often do not appear within the split of a second, they have been simmering for a while. How does the cluster fit into historical context? Given the historical context and subject of a trend cluster, what do you think the shift means? Finding key forces and drivers behind the gradual development of a trend is the aim of this question.

You can use STEEP as a tool to guide you through this process. When looking back, are there any social, technological, economic, environmental or political factors that influenced the emergence of a specific trend cluster? From a certain law being laid down that fuelled a movement or a medical invention that became a fire-starter, from a war that caused a certain effect to climate issues resulting in a specific shift. In addition, you can interview people who can look at a subject from a historical perspective, like a sociologist or an expert on the topic at hand.

"I create trend timelines which show the history and development of a certain change."

Juan Pablo Zapata Barros - Freelance Trend Researcher

QUESTION

Can you create a timeline related to a trend cluster?
Making a visual timeline can help to understand the development of a trend. Create a timeline for a trend cluster. If you do not have trend cluster yet, create a timeline for a certain topic, like feminism or capitalism.

» **What is the shift in values and needs?**
What are the main underlying values that this trend addresses? These questions are about finding the core values underlying a shift. You have already been thinking about this while clustering your manifestations and have assigned keywords to each cluster. Now it is time to double check if these are the most relevant keywords to describe the shift in values and needs. For example, the concept of living a healthy lifestyle has changed over the past decades. If you see something changing in this domain you need to pinpoint what the change is in values and needs concerning a healthy lifestyle right now as opposed to what it meant before.

*"You can scan for phenomena, walk the high streets, check out interior styles and such.
But interpreting what you have observed is the most difficult part."*

Carl Rohde - Culture Sociologist and founder of Science of the Time

You can use tools like laddering, where you once again pose the why-question to really get to the core of the motivations behind a trend cluster. You can use value models, such as Rokeach, to get inspiration for a way of putting the value shift into words. It can be helpful to check sources again and lookout for emotionally charged words used to describe a certain manifestation or look at what experts are using as ways to describe the value shift. Mark these words in your documents, make a list of them and decide on the most iconic ones that describe the shift best.

» **Who started this trend and who is spreading it?**
Who are the main creators, innovators and early adopters? These questions are about finding the key influencers of a trend cluster, which can be individuals, collectives or organisations and brands. There are always people or organisations that start a movement and others to help spread the movement. Did someone make an iconic artwork that charged a debate about a certain topic related to your trend cluster? Did someone write down their vision in a book, related to your trend cluster? Is there a brand that jumped the bandwagon first and is already implementing this trend into their strategy or communication? Check your manifestations again, discuss with others and make a list of people and companies to decide which are the most relevant to mention in your trend description. You can interview innovators to gain more insight into their way of thinking.

*"I always like to add layers to information that create added value to the information.
These layers could for instance be interviews with innovative entrepreneurs."*

Nadines Guhlich - Audience Research Lead at Soundcloud

Not only look at the frontrunners starting a movement but also try to identify certain groups within society that are early adopters. Try to define the lifestyle of people related to each of your trend clusters to get a feeling of which type of people feel attracted to this trend. You can use texts and visuals to create a mood board that describes this lifestyle. Finding key examples of inventors, frontrunners and early adopters within a trend cluster is essential because you can monitor them to see how a trend is evolving. Also knowing who they are can be crucial in the apply phase where some of them might become anchors, influencers or a target group during an innovation process.

» **Which phase is the trend in?**
Can you estimate in which stage of diffusion it is? Is it wild, emergent or already more established? These questions are about checking how emergent your trend cluster is. Especially when starting out in trend research, you might come up with more established trend clusters that are not really in an early stage anymore and are already accepted by groups of people. You might consider to drop these types of clusters because they are not future forward enough to mention to your audience. Or it can be the other way around, you might have spotted wild signs that point into a direction that is not very clear yet.

*"When you compare sources and see diverse opinions, you might have to wait a bit before
thinking and communicating about a trend, you might have spotted it in a too early stage."*

Björn Theis - Foresight Manager at Evonik

As a tool you can use the Rogers' curve and try to plot your trend clusters on it and discuss with others where they would place them. Trends placed at the start of the curve might be too upcoming and wild to mention, while others might be too mainstream. Asking yourself these questions will help you to decide to go along with a cluster, to delete it or to put it on hold for now.

» **Where can you see this trend happening already?**
What are the most relevant and significant manifestations of the trend? Can you see it happening across various sectors, regions, cultures, lifestyles and so on? Although you already made a rough selection of manifestations during the scan phase, it is now crucial to sift through these again with the core of your trend clusters in mind. Because the manifestations you will select to mention in your trend description function as important evidence to show that a trend is already happening.

> *"Always rely on evidence, the signals. Don't get lost when describing a trend and ask yourself: where did I actually see this happen?"*
>
> Hannah Lincoln - Culture Research Manager at China Youthology

Ask yourself if you have enough signals across various sectors, regions, cultures and lifestyles. If not, try to find more signals with similar values and needs across these topics. If you cannot find these easily, it tells you something about your trend cluster. Maybe it is happening mainly in a specific sector, health for example, or in one region in the world, like Asia? If you have found enough signs of change related to your trend cluster then decide on which are the most relevant and represent your cluster the best. Discuss this with others to find out which of the manifestations will help you to bring your trend cluster to life and make an interesting and inspiring storyline.

» **Which consequences can this trend have on our future quality of life?**
What could the impact on our future daily lives look like? These questions are meant to assess the impact a trend cluster might have on people's daily lives if it would spread into the majority. Can you imagine what a world would look like in five to ten years when this trend cluster might have become the norm? To think about the social implications of changes in the future trend researchers use the 'what if' question as a crucial element in their trend analysis. Though you can use your own personal imagination as a starting point, also try to find sources that showcase a vision on possible futures to have multiple perspectives on this topic. It might mean you would have to do some additional research to find out about possible future impacts of your trend cluster.

> *"During our analysis we would interview experts. If we have spotted something, say, a new technology, we try to find a world class expert to discuss it with in order to understand the impact it might have."*
>
> Björn Theis - Foresight Manager at Evonik

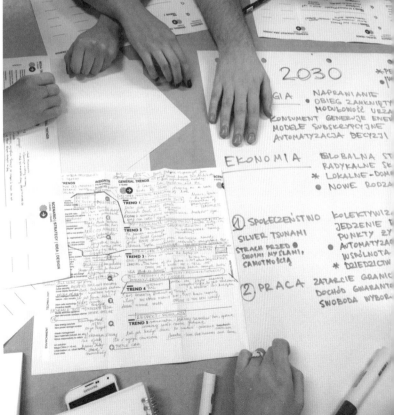

COMMUNICATION VIA STREET ART
MAKING A STATEMENT THROUGH STREETART

Hapin ess

Turi Tara

BLUE CREA-TURE

Wisdo M

TREES WOODEN WITH SOCKS BIRDS

FEELINGS

UNIVER-SALISM

ON STUFF

TREES

OLD BUILD ING

ON THE SNOW

2030

GIA   NAPRAWIANIE
         OBIEG ZAMKNIĘTY
         MODUŁOWOŚĆ URZA
KONSUMENT GENERUJE ENE
MODELE SUBSKRYPCYJNE
AUTOMATYZACJA DECYZJI

EKONOMIA   GLOBALNA ST
            RADYKALNE SK
         * LOKALNE-DOMO
         ● NOWE RODZA

① SPOŁECZEŃSTWO   KOLEKTYWIZ
   SILVER TSUNAMI   JEDZENIE
                    PUNKTY ŻY
   STRACH PRZED ●   AUTOMATYZA
   SWOIMI MYŚLAMI, WSPÓLNOTA
   SAMOTNOŚCIĄ   * DZIEDZICTW

② PRACA   ZATARCIE GRANIC
           DOCHÓD GWARANTO
           SWOBODA WYBOR

QUESTION ··

Can you validate a trend cluster?
Select one of the initial clusters and start out with asking yourself all kinds of questions about this cluster. Can you answer them immediately or not? Do you need to do extra research and scan some more? Define the type of information that is lacking and how to find it. Do the extra research and try to answer the questions again. Do you feel satisfied enough?

STAY CRITICAL

Whichever analysis format you work with, during the validation step you should always stay critical. If a detail does not really seem to resonate with your trend cluster, delete it. Read and re-read the description of your cluster with an outsider in mind to feel if your way of thinking is making enough sense.

> *"It is important to not get too subjective and be too naive and positive about a trend. For instance, when the 'sharing economy' started to emerge there were a lot of hallelujah stories out there whereas many did not mention the already observable darker sides to it."*
> Carl Rohde - Culture Sociologist and founder of Science of the Time

The validation part can strain your brains and you will certainly get tired of scanning all your sources again and doing additional research. Never let this hold you back from staying frank with yourself and push yourself to investigate even more if necessary.

> *"Analysis is not only about using tools, it is also about having an emotional intelligence, that helps you see and understand. Often I see things I don't understand immediately, but I ask more questions, above and under the subject, I really dive into it. You should be constantly curious to dig deep enough."*
> Zuzanna Skalska - Founding Partner of 360Inspiration

Being critical not only means researching more but also daring to delete. Taking a break is also part of the validation process. It will help you to stay sharp and take a look at your trend descriptions afresh. Going for a walk or doing some other physical activities in-between during analysing can help reset your brain and give a new impulse to your work. Discussing your findings so far with others is also a good way to get a new perspective on your trend descriptions. Many trend professionals are part of a team and share their findings on a regular basis with other members to gain new insights and fine-tune their trend stories.

> *"You need to analyse together because you need others to challenge you. Most of the time I check my analysis with three other people. When I'm telling someone else the trend story I understand better if the analysis and storyline is working or not."*
> Laura Wolfs - Senior Research Consultant at Point Blank International

When is it time to finish the validation part of your trend analysis? Although analysing is a continuous and iterative process that goes on day after day for any trend pro, it is also a skill to know when to stop your analysis. Unfortunately there is no winning formula to decide when it is time to quit, it is a skill you have to acquire by experience. But when you have tried to answer the validation questions from the checklist by doing additional research, discussed the outline of your trend description with others and fine-tuned the overall storyline, you are probably good to go.

> *"Analysis is also about knowing when to stop. You search, you pause, you reflect and review and do it again. You decide to explore more deeply only if you feel the direction you are headed into is relevant."*
> Kelly McKnight - Head of Culture & Trends at Join the Dots

The output of this validation process are trend descriptions that have an inspiring narrative as well as a solid backbone enriched with sources and argumentation. You can finish off the validation step by documenting the description of your trend clusters in a structured way by writing down the answers to every question and including a reference list of sources. This way you are ready for the next and last step in your analysis process: labelling your trend clusters.

STEP 3: LABEL

When you have clustered and validated your manifestations, you can move to the next and final step of analysing, which is labelling your trends. This means completing each trend storyline by capturing it in a trend name and trend image. You have to move from digging deeper to getting to the core without losing the essence of each trend cluster. Therefore a trend name and image should always capture the main value shift behind any trend cluster. The aim in the end is to leave an impression and communicate your trend clusters to your audience in a meaningful and inspiring way.

> *"It's an exercise in storytelling. Finding the most efficient way to move your trend story forward."*
>
> Rodrigo dos Reis - Consumer Trends Specialist at Zeitgeist

Every trend professional has their own preferences in labelling trends. From being very visual and mood focused to a more functional and down-to-earth approach. Either way, text and imagery have to show a consistent and balanced style. By the way you label trends you can showcase your personal trend signature. Checking how others label their trends provides useful inspiration to find your own style preference. In this section you be brought up to date on various ways of labelling trends, starting with naming them and ending with visualising them.

NAME IT

First up you are going to think of a name to label each one of your trend clusters. This is important because a name gives a sneak peek into the main underlying values and needs behind a cluster. It also helps your audience to remember and communicate with others about a trend. Sometimes you can coin a trend by being the first to name it in a certain way. Trend names can even make it to everyday language like Faith Popcorn coined 'cocooning' in the eighties.

> *"Think of it as the cover of a magazine with one killer headline about a story which is compelling as well as meaningful, that's how you should articulate your trend themes."*
>
> Sam Shaw - Head of Insight at Canvas8

To come up with a meaningful and at the same time catchy trend name requires copywriting skills. Trend agencies often employ editors whose main task is to compose an attractive text for each trend cluster, including a trend name. As a trend researcher you should be able to communicate abstract and complex topics in an accessible and straightforward manner so people can relate to it. There are many ways to name a trend. If you are not sure yet about your own style preferences it helps to review how others are naming their trends. Trend professionals often share (parts of) their trend research for free so you can check their trend overviews and see how they name their trends.

> *"We use names like Let's Play, Doing It Together and Precious Time. I feel that a trend name should represent the people and their needs, that the names represent something a consumer could have said. "*
>
> Kelly McKnight - Head of Culture & Trends at Join the Dots

QUESTION ···

What is your preference in name styles?
Go online and visit various websites of trend agencies and trend freelancers to check how they name their trend clusters.

» Which trend names resonate with you? Why do they?
» Which names do not stick with you at all? Why don't they?
» What does this tell you about your own style preferences?

Looking at how others name their trend clusters shows some interesting overlaps in ways of naming. Often a trend name consists of one or two words maximum. Many trend professionals like to use language in a figurative way and combine existing words into a new one, like 'Flawsome' (TrendWatching), 'Wonderlust' (MARE), 'Transcreation' (Fontys, Ambiente) or Flexurbinity (Fontys, DDW). It also seems many have a love for alliteration and use the same letter at the beginning of every word in the name, for example Capacity Capture (TrendWatching), Cool Curation (MARE), Tangible Tech (Fontys, Ambiente) and Stringed Society (Fontys, DDW). Some choose to use local language to name their trends, others use English so it can be understood worldwide. Decide on one language for consistency and do not use a different kind of language for every cluster.

Many trend professionals also use a trend tagline in addition to a trend name. This is a memorable phrase that clarifies a trend cluster by using just one sentence. This is useful as a teaser in reports and presentations because you can clarify a trend cluster a bit more without revealing everything. For example, the tagline of the trend Wonderlust is 'seeing the extraordinary in the ordinary' (MARE), the tagline for the trend Betterment is 'the universal quest for self-improvement (TrendWatching) and for a trend named Rewilding it is 'seeking to restore the lost values of nature' (Canvas8). Browse through examples of trend agencies to find inspiration on taglines to see which type you find the most attractive.

That others work this way does not mean you will have to, find your own unique style. To start naming your own trends it helps to create a mind map for each cluster putting the values in the middle and branching out by thinking of interesting ways to rename these values. Invite others and brainstorm together to collect more interesting words to label your trend clusters with. Make use of a thesaurus if your creative juices run dry. To finish, create a shortlist of names and taglines you like the best and test them with others to observe their reactions and make your final choice.

> *"Getting consensus on the trend name is a team effort. I always present a name and description to my team because by discussing it I always see something I didn't see before which makes the end result different but better."*
>
> Nelson Pinheiro - Assistant Professor of Trends Studies and Cultural Management at the University of Lisbon

SHOW, DON'T TELL

Now that you have your trend names in order, it is time to think of key visuals to represent each of your trend clusters. As the saying goes, a picture is worth a thousand words. Talking about trends and futures can stay really abstract, visuals help us to imagine possible futures by conveying moods and feelings related to the trends. Also, everyone processes information in different ways either via text or via visuals. That is why a trend researcher should be able to communicate trends not only in text but also in visuals.

> *"I feel storytelling is an essential part of educating people in which future direction to move, so I spend a lot of time finding the right high-resolution images and videos for my presentations. I use only one word per slide to amplify the image."*
>
> Niels van der Burg - Global Category Insights Manager at Asics

Selecting or creating images that represent your trend clusters is a skill acquired by experience. Next to copywriters, trend agencies often employ image editors whose main task is to search and collect images and adjust them for proper use in reports or presentations. You do not have to be educated in art or design to be able to find the most fitting images, although it helps to have a feel for visual aesthetics.

> *"I really like to use visual metaphors as much as I can to make trends more clear and to find pictures that bring the signals and trends even more to life."*
>
> Hannah Lincoln - Culture Research Manager at China Youthology

There are many ways to visualise a trend and the same goes for trend visuals as for trend names: if you are not sure yet about your own style preferences it helps to review how others are visualising their trends. As mentioned before trend professionals often share (parts of) their trend research for free so you can check their trend overviews to see how they visualise their trends.

QUESTION ··

What is your preference in visual styles?
Go online and visit various websites of trend agencies and trend freelancers to check how they visualise their trend clusters.

» Which trend visuals resonate with you? Why do they?
» Which visuals do not stick with you at all? Why don't they?
» What does this tell you about your own style preferences?

Looking at how others visualise their trend clusters provides some interesting pointers on how to visualise your trends. In the end it all comes down to deciding on the type of images you would like to use. Do you want to use existing images or create your own? Creating your own images has the advantage that you do not have to worry about copyrights. Also you can model and shape these images in whichever way you want them to be. A disadvantage is that it can be very time consuming to create your own trend imagery or costly to have them created.

"I take a lot of photos and videos. I like using my own pictures from field work, which are very real and candid."

Rodrigo dos Reis - Consumer Trends Specialist at Zeitgeist

Finding and using relevant existing images is not so difficult because there are plenty of visual offline and online resources, from design blogs to art magazines. You can also be inspired by visual oriented trend agencies. Do not forget to take a look again at the visual materials you have collected during the scanning phase, maybe you can use some of it at this stage. Always make sure to only use high-resolution images for a professional look. Remember to always credit every image you use. The disadvantage of using existing material can be that you have to pay for copyrights when you want to publish these images.

"I use Tumblr a lot as source to find images, I follow a few nice Tumblr blogs that show and share great images. When I go to exhibitions I write down the names of artists whose work I feel I can use to represent a trend."

Loui Sampaio - Former exchange student at Fontys Minor Trend Watching

Do you want to use metaphorical or literal images? Using metaphorical visuals to represent your clusters makes them more exciting and interesting. They can show the mood and feeling of a cluster better than a very literal image could. Therefore it is best to not use stock photos because these are mostly soulless pictures. Ask yourself what a trend symbolises and stands for, what does it look and feel like? It helps to brainstorm with others to find inspiring metaphors.

"For my Spring '18 presentation I used a photo of a pile of fake life vests at the Turkish coast. With these pictures I tried to create awareness and understanding how to connect socio-cultural trends to what's happening in the world around us."

Niels van der Burg - Global Category Insights Manager at Asics

On the other hand, being literal can also be a style choice depending on your key audience. Many business sectors do not have a visual oriented culture and are more text and number driven. They might be overwhelmed by trends visualised in an abstract way. In this case, a functional approach can be more effective where literal images of manifestations you have spotted are shown, like new products and services.

"I use a lot of pictures that feature manifestations like new locations and new products. These are very functional pictures, I fear that when pictures are too abstract some people might not understand these the way I want them too."

Juan Pablo Zapata Barros - Freelance Trend Researcher

TOOL: MOOD BOARD

Visual oriented trend researchers create trend mood boards for each of their clusters, which function as trend inspiration sheets with an arranged collection of accurately selected images to visualise the idea behind a trend. You can make analogue or digital mood boards and use any image source you like. To start visualising your own trends you can create mood boards for each cluster. Map out several trend related images on your computer or on a table or wall.

Invite others and brainstorm together about composition and combination, how do these images complement each other? Experiment with combinations by pairing images and add or delete visuals to find exciting combinations that communicate the core of your trend cluster the best. In the end it is most important to be consistent in your visual language and style, whichever style you choose.

INTERVIEW | Djenny Brugmans & Nanon Soeters

Djenny Brugmans and Nanon Soeters
Partners at Rozenbrood

How would you describe your ways of working?
"We are trendwatchers using today's visual culture to depict tomorrow's world. As we have a background in art history and graphic design, we use our ability to interpret images to communicate with our clients about trends. We also try to picture the future using our knowledge about management and our experience in educating people about trends."

Why focus on images?
"Images have two sides to us, they are a source of trend information and they are a way to communicate about trends. Images trigger a different part of the brain, a presentation with bullet points has a different effect on an audience than a presentation packed with images. We feel images work very well in telling the story of the future, because it is non-existent yet. Visuals help people to imagine possible futures."

What defines a good image?
"It all depends on what you want to achieve with the images in your trend presentations and who your audience are. Consider the use of showing the visuals. Would the receiver understand them the way you intended?"

What type of images do you often use?
"Most people are used to stock photography but we feel these show a polished version of the world. We like to use more authentic images to represent a value shift, ranging from art and design visuals to more realistic and down-to-earth photos from newspapers and websites."

Do you create your own images?
"We almost never create our own images but use found images in trend presentations. Using already existing visuals validates that a trend is really happening. Also it is very time consuming to create your own images."

How do you integrate visuals in your presentations?
"We visualise our final analysis by using a lot of images in our presentation. Often we use one to two images on one slide with keywords next to them. We always credit the artists of the visuals we use. When we publish trend books we contact the creators of the images to ask permission to use them. We also try not to use the images in a way that the artist did not intend, so we always research the meaning behind the visual."

Do you select visuals to fit your audience?
"Yes, because in the end we want to inspire and activate our clients. We once worked for a professional network of pastry chefs, which is an audience not used to trend presentations at all. So we tried to visualise each trend in a way it would relate to their profession using various images of cakes, bread, chocolate and baking tools in literal and metaphorical ways. This worked out very well in getting the trends across to this audience."

TREND OVERVIEW

The output of the analysis phase is a trend overview which shows your trend clusters in an organised and concise way. This overview summarises your trend knowledge in a simplified and easy to understand way. This index shows others which trends are relevant right now and enables you to start a conversation about them. The overview serves as a starting point during the next phase to decide which trends are most relevant for a specific case.

The overview also helps to keep up with how trends evolve and move. Trends are dynamic and their directions change, so the overview is not set in stone and serves as a snapshot of your current trends clusters. You have to keep on monitoring trends and refine them, delete ones that fade out or become mainstream and add new emerging ones. When new manifestations do not fit naturally into your trend overview then things start to get interesting again.

"We have an overview that consists of fourteen trends. This is a useful starting point for any of our client's questions. It is a process to develop this set of trends, you drop some of the themes, you add some, it is an ongoing process."

Kelly McKnight - Head of Culture & Trends at Join the Dots

To create an overview it helps if it covers only one page so that the clusters are visible at a glance. A trend overview usually holds the names of every trend cluster and also a summary of the key values and needs. You could add iconic visuals for each trend including the trend levels and connections between them. The overall diagram could be called a trend overview, a trend map, a trend index or any suitable name. The overview is the skeleton of your trend research. For your own reference it is practical to have a document with background information for every trend cluster. It describes the results of the validation stage and functions as the backbone of your overview.

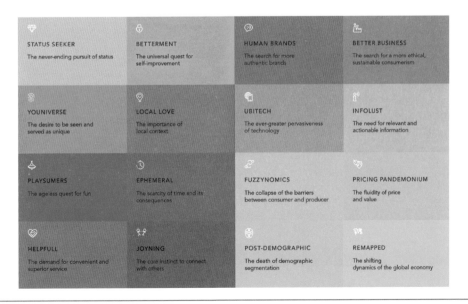

An example of a trend overview by TrendWatching.

+ SUMMARY

» The analyse phase is about giving meaning to your trend spots.

» An analysis is like piecing a puzzle where you connect the dots in unexpected ways.

» Analysing can be done in a structured three step way: cluster, validate, label.

CLUSTER

» Cluster is about grouping manifestations that represent the same underlying emerging needs and values by asking why it is happening.

» Clustering can be done by using tools like laddering.

VALIDATE

» Validation of your clusters is needed to really understand the emergence of trends.

» You can ask yourself specific questions to structure your validation and make it complete and coherent.

LABEL

» By labelling the clusters with an iconic name and visual you bring the trend to life for others.

» You create a trend overview showing every cluster on it.

+ WANT TO KNOW MORE?

Eager to learn more about the analysis phase of trend research?
Here you can find some suggestions for further reading, watching and clicking.
This is a selection of a vast array of sources. You can find more information at
www.howtoresearchtrends.com.

LADDERING ···

» Understanding Consumer Decision Making, a book by Thomas Reynolds and Jerry Olson
» Doing Social Psychology Research, a book by Glennis Breakwell

MIND MAPPING TOOLS ···

For digital mind mapping you can use tools like Mindmeister, Bubbl, Padlet or
many others that are out there. Good old-fashioned paper sheets still work their
magic too.

NAME INSPIRATION ···

For inspiration on the name game of trend clusters you can check sites of
for example TrendWatching, Canvas8 and Ambientetrends.

VISUAL INSPIRATION ···

Standard search engines rarely provide the needed visual inspiration that goes beyond
stock photography so check other sources, for example the ones listed below:

» Websites by visual oriented trend agencies like Trend Union or Nelly Rodi.
» Websites by more functional oriented trend agencies like TrendWatching or Canvas8.
» Street style blogs like The Sartorialist or Cobra Snake to find images of people.
» Design sites like Trendland, Design Inspiration and Designboom.
» Material and finishes sites like Materia.nl
» Use the search function on visual platforms like Tumblr.
» Check the APA-style guidelines on how to cite images.

#5

APPLY

INNOVATE OR DIE!

So many trends! How can these be applied during an innovation process? In this chapter you will define a trend scope and curate your trend research in a tailor-made way. You will finish the trend research process by translating trend insights into future-proof ideas.

X TOPICS

X INTRO

Insights in emerging values and needs serve as a foundation for vision building and decision-making because trend research draws the attention to future challenges and opportunities for any type of organisation. During the last decades the domain of trend research expanded from detecting and analysing change to also helping others put it to use. The apply phase of trend research is about communicating your findings in a made-to-measure way so others can decide to act on it or not.

> *"My job is not to develop new business models or decide on shapes and styles. I show future directions and facilitate in how to translate these into innovation activities."*

Claudia Lieshout - Creative Director Lifestyle Trends
at Philips Design

This chapter will help you to apply your findings in a tailored way for any type of innovation process. You will first define a scope for the project at hand. Then you will be informed about various ways to curate and communicate trends in a relevant way. And finally you will learn to translate trends into innovative ideas. Examples of how different types of companies are applying trends are spread out through this chapter. Be inspired by the trend process of sportswear brand Asics, chemicals supplier Evonik, electronics company Philips, the Dutch Ministry of General Affairs and online music platform Soundcloud.

TREND INSPIRED INNOVATION

Trend research delivers insights about directions of change which can be applied by organisations to adjust their current offerings. Whether you are a researcher, a designer, a marketer, a policy maker, a student or a professional and working in a commercial or public domain, trend research helps you to align with people's changing needs and wants. By using the trend values as guidance throughout the innovation process you create value in the end for consumers, citizens and everyone around the globe.

> *"If you don't use trends in your concepting process the innovation achieved will only meet actual demands in the market, which only have a small growth potential."*
> Jakob Sutmuller - Senior Lecturer Concepting & Business Innovation at Fontys ILS

People are action oriented, they like to apply knowledge to change their circumstances (Bell, 2003). Change is at the core of innovation, but what is innovation exactly? As mentioned in chapter two, according to Rogers (2003) an innovation is an idea, practice or object that is perceived as new. This means innovation covers a broad spectrum from a new strategy or policy to a new kind of behaviour, a new product or service. Trends and innovation are often linked to each other. While trend research is about detecting and understanding change, an innovation process is aimed at creating change. The output of trend research is a powerful starting point for innovation. Trend insights can be used as a springboard to act upon, whether you want to create a competitive edge in business or address a societal issue. It enables you to develop visionary and future-proof solutions that create impact and improve people's quality of life.

> *"Is it important to innovate? Not for the sake of innovation itself but you need to innovate to keep track with the changing environment and people's needs."*
> Erica Bol - Change Maker at Teach the Future

To be able to change and innovate requires an open mind-set during the process of innovation. Recognising the potential of a changing environment, reflecting on it and embracing uncertainty are key during this process. Trend insights open up people's mind-sets about a transitioning world and their position in it.

> *"Trend research provides new insights that challenge the status quo and shows an open horizon with previously unidentified challenges and opportunities."*
> Cornelia Daheim - Principal of Future Impact

TREND INSPIRED INNOVATION EXAMPLES

The following examples give you an idea where translations of trend values can lead.

"We provide different angles on youth mind-sets via our trends and the implications these can have for brands. For instance a trend in China a couple of years ago was about dating less out of obligation and more out of exploration. You can apply this type of trend in various ways from developing products that can be used by couples to how you are portraying couples in campaigns."

Hannah Lincoln - Culture Research Manager at China Youthology

"We worked for a beer brand on a project about alcohol moderation for millennials. Our insights are used to support them in telling stories, developing campaigns and creating press releases."

Sam Shaw - Head of Insight at Canvas8

"How do I apply a trend about recession proof consuming for a soft drink brand, a telecom brand and a luxury brand? They are all facing this same trend but the strategy on how to apply this trend in their domain and for their brand can be very different. The soft drink brand can give you more for less, so bigger deals. A telecom brand can provide specific timeslots in which you could call for free. Exclusive luxury brands can counter this trend and communicate that they will continue to deliver the same quality for the same price guaranteeing you high quality as always. Same trend, different approaches."

Franklin Ozekhom - Pop Culture Strategist at TINK

"In a project we once pointed out that next to an increase of a population living on lower budgets there was an increase in awareness of sustainability in the public sector. Our client combined these trend insights and developed a cheap solution to purify water for their African market. A trend based project can be a catalyst, there should always be someone at the client side who is an ambassador and wants a certain shift or idea to come together, and can push it from the inside."

Cornelia Daheim - Principal of Future Impact

Nowadays innovation is often seen as something worth pursuing and has a mostly positive connotation to it. Nevertheless it is also necessary to not focus blindly on change. Take a pause and reflect on what is worth to preserve and maintain too. You do not have to change everything radically because change can create better worlds but also worse ones. An innovation process is therefore also about deciding whether to act or not, where deciding not to act is also an action in itself (Bell, 2003).

> *"Managers often have high expectation of innovation processes. They should not be too focused on just the innovation part and lose sight of their functioning business foundations."*
>
> Tim Schuurman - Partner at DesignThinkers Group

Trend inspired innovation is not an individual process. The trend researcher's role is to provide trend insights as a foundation to build upon innovation. Working in multidisciplinary teams is the preferred way of sharing trend insights and making them actionable for others to amplify. As a trend researcher you combine your skills in trend analysis with the creative skills of others by collaborating with concept developers, design thinkers and innovation strategists during the translation step. This way you join forces and make sure that underlying trend values will always serve as the foundation of creating innovations.

> *"Always apply trends together with your client and work in multidisciplinary teams that have various people on board, like decision makers, marketers, sales reps, R&D people and designers."*
>
> Zuzanna Skalska - Founding Partner of 360Inspiration

APPLY STEPS

Your general overview of trends serves as a foundation for applying trends to a specific question or problem. Although in practice innovation processes have an iterative and nonlinear dynamic, you can follow certain steps to use your trend insights as fire-starters in this process. To help you embark on this exciting last phase of in trend research, applying trends is divided in three steps: Scope, Communicate and Translate. On the next pages you will dive into every step and learn how to use these steps to provide a trend-based springboard for others to move forward.

> *"It's not always obvious for organisations how trends are related to their business question. As a trend researcher you need to help them see these relations."*
>
> Laura Wolfs - Senior Research Consultant at Point Blank International

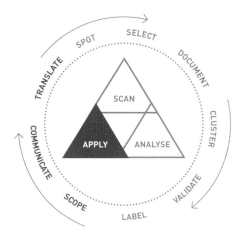

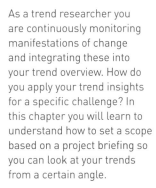

STEP 1: SCOPE ➜

As a trend researcher you are continuously monitoring manifestations of change and integrating these into your trend overview. How do you apply your trend insights for a specific challenge? In this chapter you will learn to understand how to set a scope based on a project briefing so you can look at your trends from a certain angle.

STEP 2: COMMUNICATE ➜

Based on the scope you decide on how to communicate your trends. Which factors do you need to take into consideration to adapt your trend story to a specific audience or challenge? In this chapter you will be updated on trend storytelling and the pros and cons of various types of trend deliverables.

STEP 3: TRANSLATE

The last step in the apply phase for a trend researcher is helping others to make a first step towards change and innovation. In this chapter you will learn about various tools and activities to implement and translate trends into future-proof ideas.

TRENDS & ASICS

Niels van der Burg - Global Category Insights Manager at Asics

"A product is only one way for a brand like Asics to translate a trend. Trends have a much broader scope and should be applicable to our whole company. You can use the same trend but have a different interpretation per department. The goal is to make trends practical for every person in our company. In the beginning of my career I created quite fluffy, mood focused presentations. For our design team that was workable but for our sales team it was not at all. I try to be as inspirational and informative for every one of our departments. I like to give them a wakeup call and show different opportunities via my trend overviews. The overall major trends stay the same for a longer period of time, like lack of trust or stress in society. Those are applicable to whatever audience you have. I translate those in a tailor-made way for each of our departments. For example, when I create a presentation for our merchandise or sales teams, I talk about the rise of chat bots and how to interpret this as a new sales opportunity. But for our design team I wouldn't go that deep into chat bots, but I would dive into biomimicry and sustainability.

I work for ASICS, so the goal is obviously to sell performance and lifestyle products. But being a brand nowadays transcends this and is also about creating social value. Adding value actually resonates with the foundation of the ASICS company: creating sportswear products that enable people to live a healthier and happier life. If you know how to translate trends you can reach your consumers better as a brand. A trend like distrust means that people value up-close and personal contact more. This is relevant for our marketing department as well as our sales department. As a company it is really about showing your added value to consumers who are looking for likeminded brands."

STEP 1: SCOPE

The previous chapters guided you in doing unfocused trend research and cover a wide range of topics to create a trend overview. Now someone, for example a client or a colleague, comes along and asks you to apply these trends to a specific challenge. This means you will have to look at your trend overview from a new perspective. People have different reasons to seek for trend information and will use it in various circumstances. Understanding their perspective is what this first step in the apply phase is about.

> *"Often colleagues walk up to me asking something along the lines of 'can you do some trends about topic x?'"*
>
> Claudia Lieshout - Creative Director Lifestyle Trends at Philips Design

For every project there is a so-called client. You might be an employee working within an organisation on a trend driven project and have internal colleagues as your clients. Or maybe you are hired as an external trend consultant by an organisation to assist in applying trends for a specific project. Perhaps you are a student working on a project where you apply trends for a fictional or real-life client? Maybe you are working on a personal project and you are your own client? In any of these cases, the one who is commissioning the project is a client and this term will be used throughout this chapter to refer to this person.

So many trends, which one(s) should an organisation or brand tap into? Understanding the scope will guide you from your broad overview of trends to a curated selection of relevant trend insights for the challenge at hand. In this phase of trend research it is not about being complete but about selecting information in a way that a client can use it throughout their innovation process.

> *"I always embed trend research in my client's context. Companies know a lot about what works for them and do not have to hop on every trend bandwagon."*
>
> Laura Wolfs - Senior Research Consultant at Point Blank International

TREND BRIEFING

To be able to curate your trend findings you need to ask a client a lot of questions and get to the core of their challenge. Start out with setting up a briefing, preferably a face-to-face meeting at your client's work space. This will give you more insight into their work ethics and culture. Set the agenda of the meeting and prepare a list with key questions you want to ask. During the briefing listen well and dare to ask for explanations if you do not understand fully what your client is trying to say. Be the one to structure the conversation and do not get hung up on details. Manage expectations by giving a clear sense of who you are and what you bring to the table.

> *"Never just copy the client's briefing. You always have to dig deeper to truly understand the question of your client and find the right point of departure."*
>
> Pernille Kok-Jensen - Connectivity Director at MARE

You can structure your trend briefing with the proposed topics in the following briefing checklist. Add anything that might be related to your specific project.

Meeting 10/00

➢ Goal of the project =
creating an innovative leisure
concept for senior citizens

TREND BRIEFING CHECKLIST

» Why are we here?
» What is the main question?
» What is the internal context?
» What are specifications of the challenge?
» On which level does the client want to apply trends?
» What is the trend sensitivity of the client?
» What is the desired deliverable?
» What type of collaboration does the client prefer?
» What are the budget and timings?

» **Why are we here?**
What is the main reason the client has asked you for trend input? Can they give you some background information on this?

» **What is the main question?**
What is the main question your client wants to have answered or problem they want to get solved? What kind of value or effect would they like to create? What will it take to make the client happy at the end of this project? Try to uncover the core question.

» **What is the internal context?**
Behind most requests lies a hidden web of internal politics. Make sure to find out who makes the decisions, who are the stakeholders and what they mean for the success of the project. Who does your client need to convince in the end? The audience of your deliverables is probably much bigger than only your main contact person.

» **What are specifications of the challenge?**
Is the core question related to a specific topic they want you to focus on, for example a region, culture, target group or sector? Do they want to be inspired and updated on general trends, do they need help in deciding which trends to tap into or do they want to create something innovative based on trends?

» **On which level does the client want to apply trends?**
Trend insights can be used, for example, as input for creating a new strategy or for deciding on a style preference. Which route does your client want to take? Do they need input for policy, strategy, products, services, marketing, communication, design or style?

» **What is the trend sensitivity of the client?**
How sensitive to trends is the client? Where would they position themselves on the innovation curve of Rogers? Are they more of a follower or an innovator? Are they familiar with trends and have they applied them before or are they new in this arena? How do they keep themselves up to date on trends, are they visiting trade shows, reading certain magazines or doing anything else to be informed? Find out where the added value of your trend research lies.

» **What is the desired deliverable?**
How and with whom does the client want to share the results? Do they want you to share the findings via a report, a presentation, a workshop, a video or in any other way? Why do they prefer this specific deliverable?

» **What type of collaboration does the client prefer?**
Would they like you to take the lead, mainly work independently and show the results at the end? Or do they like to collaborate, be a project partner and get involved throughout the process?

» **What are the budget and timings?**
Clients usually want everything and they want it fast. Help them to find their focus and to understand that more or faster is not always better. What timeframe is the client thinking of? What kind of budget do they have available? Clearly communicate the consequences of each choice for timings and budget.

The output of a trend briefing is a debrief with a clear demarcation of the project scope. Formulate your vision on the client's challenge and send it to the client to double check if you have understood correctly. It sometimes can be hard to keep track of the main question when diving into a project. When in doubt on how to communicate or translate your trends always check the debrief. Bear in mind that your role as a researcher is to stay objective and neutral with regards to the client's challenge. Do not get pulled along the client's personal preferences or agenda too much. Provide them with a fresh perspective on their challenge.

"There are always political dimensions and limitations. You should be aware of these in order for your trend recommendations to be as useful as possible."
Rodrigo dos Reis - Consumer Trends Specialist at Zeitgeist

QUESTION

Can you create a list of questions for a briefing?
Think of the challenge and come up with as many questions as you can regarding this challenge. Check with others which questions the challenge evokes with them and add these to your list. Check information prior to meeting your client, for example their website or annual reports. Does it contain information that already answers some of your questions? Delete these from the list.

TRENDS & EVONIK
Björn Theis - Foresight Manager at Evonik

"Evonik is a business to business company in specialty chemicals. For example, plexiglass is an Evonik invention. We also produce additives for animal food, and coatings and lightweight materials for cars, planes and ships. I work at Creavis, which is the strategic innovation unit of Evonik. It focuses on innovation projects that support Evonik's growth and sustainability strategies. Our mission in corporate foresight is to inform the corporation about new developments, innovation opportunities and risks.

In order to reach our goals, we collaborate with so-called foresight partners who are colleagues from different departments within Evonik, like human resources, strategy or production. This way of working gives us an interdisciplinary perspective and a heterogeneous view. We organise workshops over the course of a year in different cities for these partners and they can spend ten working days on innovation topics of their choice. When we work with trends we think of it as a funnel going from a broad topic like the privatisation of space to the perspective of Evonik. At first people at Evonik might think: we are not building space ships, why should we venture in that direction? But when you think about it more there are opportunities to be found. We can make additives, coatings and build lightweight materials that can be used in space ships.

We organise workshops with the foresight partners where everyone can spill out ideas on emerging topics they feel might be relevant for Evonik from the second space age to changes in immigration. Then we do a round-about where we discuss, delete and add ideas. In the end we might have twenty so-called action fields wherein it is feasible to think about the development of new products related to the business of Evonik. These become our innovation areas. A researcher would then get around three months' time to really dig into an innovation area, read research studies, travel to talk to experts and visit related conferences.

The deliverable is usually a report and presentation for the management team of Creavis that tells them what we found out and what our recommendations are for Evonik. Management decides if we should look further into it. If so, then we do another round of research and decide if we really get into the process of building prototypes and do lab research. This is when my job as foresight manager ends and others in the company take over."

STEP 2: COMMUNICATE

Based on the scope you can now decide on how to communicate your trends in a way that fits your client's challenge. This means adapting your general trend overview to the project at hand and create a relevant storyline and tailor-made deliverables. The role of the trend researcher involves being a curator during this step of the process. You will decide on how to build a narrative so your client understands the risks and opportunities the trends provide for their challenge.

> *"In these times of overload it is not the problem for my clients to find information but to select the most relevant information."*
>
> Ksenia Penkina Lery - CEO of Trendsquire

In the end the goal is to help your client find an answer to their question and your trend communication should always serve this purpose. By presenting trend insights in a made-to-measure way the core of the trend stories should help others to decide which direction to take or to avoid. Impactful communication makes your trends more meaningful to and actionable for others. During your trend briefing you have picked up on things, such as the client's internal culture, their trend sensitivity and other factors shaping your clients daily work processes. Now it is your turn to see in which ways you can surprise, challenge or reassure your client.

> *"If you want your trends to resonate with me it has to have a structured storyline and tell me about the impact a trend has and what it means for our brand."*
>
> Nadines Guhlich - Audience Research Lead at Soundcloud

COMMUNICATION APPROACH

Think about the way to approach your trend communication. For instance when a client's culture is very open and non-hierarchical you can be more daring and provocative in your tone of voice and type of deliverables. When it is the other way around, it is best to provide clients with a more reassuring perspective and show lots of proof that a trend is already happening. When a client has a high trend sensitivity you will have to find a way to surprise them, for example by carefully selecting examples of a trend that go beyond the sources they would normally use. When, on the other hand, a client has a low trend sensitivity you would have to explain more about your research process and show concrete and practical examples within their industry. This often means that your trend communication is a balancing act between being inspiring and bringing a fresh perspective versus making things relevant and actionable for a specific challenge. How to find the right balance? You can use the checklist on trend communication to help you think about your communication approach.

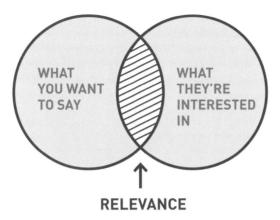

RELEVANCE

The sweetspot of trend communication.

TREND COMMUNICATION CHECKLIST

» Scope
» Audience
» Level of interaction
» Tone of voice
» Form

» **Scope**
Do not forget the scope of a project. What is the main question and how can your style of communication help in answering it for your client? Try to keep this in the back of your mind.

» **Audience**
Who will you be communicating with? Who are you going to speak to, either live or via text, video or other means of communication? What are their interests and what do they need to take from your research?

» **Level of interaction**
Looking at the type of client and the audience, would you like to have a low level of interaction and use a send-receiver approach or does a more active and engaging approach fit your client better?

» **Tone of voice**
Is your client more on the emotional side or the rational side of the spectrum? Think of the implications for your storytelling style. Would you use a formal versus informal approach, visuals versus graphs and symbolic expressions versus concrete wordings?

» **Form**

What is the desired output? This can take various forms, from a presentation to a report and from a video to a trend tour. Do you feel the required deliverable fits the client or would you propose a different set of deliverables? This is very dependent on the available budget too.

DELIVERABLES

Trend output can come in different shapes and styles. Let's take a closer look at popular types of trend output and their strengths and weaknesses. This will help you to decide which communication deliverables fits a project at hand the best. The different forms of output are arranged starting with the more passive and sender-focused deliverables to more engaging and active output. Combining different types of deliverables is also possible and often done by trend researchers.

> *"Depending on what a client wants to achieve our output ranges from reports and films, giving presentations and workshops, recreating environments to developing iPad apps."*
>
> Sam Shaw - Head of Insight at Canvas8

Trend reports

A trend report is a way to give an in-depth description of several trends. It allows you to use visuals and text and the chosen layout assists in getting the message across. You can deliver a report in a hardcopy or digital format. The latter allows you to integrate hyperlinks so readers can check original sources or videos related to the trends. You can also add trend implications for the specific client's case and integrate trend advice into the report. Reports, especially digital ones, are easy to share with others. On the other hand, reports tend to disappear in desk drawers or desktop folders because they not always bring the trends to life enough.

> *"We create digital trend books which our client can access online. This form allows us to put links, videos and other multimedia content inside."*
>
> Ksenia Penkina Lery - CEO of Trendsquire

Trend videos

Audio-visual material can really bring trends to life. It helps the viewer to understand the trend mood and become more immersed in the story. Videos can be watched on demand at any preferred time and are easy to share with others. They can also be combined easily with other communication forms like presentations. In today's visually driven culture it is a requirement that the video is shot and edited professionally which requires a certain budget. Although a video can be engaging it tends to stay passive in viewing. Read more on creating a trend video in the special section.

> *"We collaborate with freelance videographers to create movies which are immersive, evoke emotion and put human behaviour at their centre."*
>
> Sam Shaw - Head of Insight at Canvas8

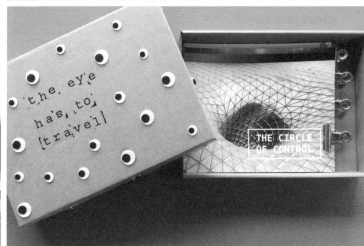

TREND VIDEOS
Heather Vescent - Futurist and founder of The Purple Tornado

"I have always liked to think in a lyrical, poetic way to communicate my thoughts. That's probably why I am now focused on expressing the feeling of being in the future through film. Film is an engaging medium, it allows you to travel through time and identify with the characters easily. This also makes film powerful because it can have a big influence on people's decision making.

Budget wise a film is more expensive than a report or presentation deck because the process of making it takes longer and you need to hire a film crew. I feel that the more polished a film is the more plausible it will seem to people. If a video lacks professionalism this will reflect on the ideas showcased in it.

A written futures report often gives an abstract big picture view, while a movie is very concrete and zooms in on people's interactions in a possible future. I write the script by myself and while writing is a solo activity, filming is teamwork. I often have a crew of over twenty people, such as actors and a cameraman, and they all bring in different energies, chaos and magic. While shooting the script, it is influenced by the people who bring the script to life. And until we get to the final cut there's a lot of changes happening to the storyline in the editing phase too.

I like to work with realistic people and put them in scenarios that show normal everyday behaviour like eating, working, meeting with friends. These are activities we have done for decades and these moments are relevant for everyone today but the way these moments are executed might change in the future. Although my films show new technologies I focus mainly on the human perspective and how tech augments humanity. I want to communicate what the future possibilities are in a pure way. I don't want to use it as a marketing instrument and manipulate viewers, I aim to open their minds."

TRENDS & PHILIPS

Claudia Lieshout - Creative Director Lifestyle Trends at Philips Design

"In order for me to showcase our human-centred trend insights, communication is key. There is no time to philosophise too much about the future; action has to be taken, decisions have to be made. At Philips Design we might have been a bit too vague and visual in the past with our presentations, while our CEO's demanded three slides with a pie chart. You really need to understand your audience when presenting trends and adjust and tweak your trend story to cater to their needs. My audience often consists of experts in health systems and I have to surprise them with my insights and at the same time show them I'm an expert too and understand the health system.

You can make beautiful and comprehensive trend reports, but most colleagues won't read them because they experience a lack of time. At the design department we have to service colleagues in a way that they will read the reports. That's why we came up with a format that you can read within 10 minutes. We also created trend cards, which have a short description of a trend and a trigger question, for instance: what if... we all become responsible for our own health? This process was really educational for us, because it forced us to come up with different ways of presenting our trend findings.

We often finish our trend projects with a workshop. During these workshops the focus is on specific topics, such as pregnant women who are expecting their first child. Or we plot our findings on a health continuum from healthy to getting sick to feeling better again. During the years we have developed a trend to innovation approach that fits our company and our business challenges."

Trend presentations

Trend researchers are often asked to present their trend insights live for small to large audiences. A presentation is suitable to bring a group of people up to date and inspire them in a short period of time. It also allows the audience to ask questions and interact with the trend researcher during or after the presentation. Presentations ask for a more visual approach to really immerse your audience. The presentation deck can be shared afterwards if needed. Presentations have the disadvantage of being volatile and not very action oriented. People tend to go on with their daily business afterwards.

> *"We use Sway to build a visual narrative for each of our trends. It can contain all kinds of information like photographs, quotes and social media snippets."*
> Kelly McKnight - Head of Culture & Trends at Join the Dots

Trend consultations

You can arrange a personal meeting with your client and some of their stakeholders to exchange views on trends. You can show your trend overview and get a conversation going about the trends. This is a more exclusive way of sharing trend insights and very tailor-made because the participants can easily ask anything they like. The downside of a personal consult is that it is not easy to share with others, the information stays with the participants only.

> "I like to start a dialogue by asking clients: what is your key take-out of this trend? Can you apply it to your business? What will you do differently tomorrow based on this trend?"
>
> Carl Rohde - Culture Sociologist and founder of Science of the Time

Trend tours

An interactive and lively way to share trend information is via trend tours. Participants are guided by a trend researcher along a variety of concrete trend examples. The researcher explains the broader trend context of each specific example. Tours can be held inside, for example at trade shows or outside: a neighbourhood trend tour for instance. Participants can interact with the researcher and talk to people they meet during the tour, like designers or store owners. Trend tours can be done within an hour to a full day, depending on the area to cover. This way of sharing trend insights is limited in the amount of participants and cannot be shared easily with others afterwards.

Trend workshops

Trend workshops are often organised when a client not only wants to know about the latest trends but also wants to take a first step into translating and thinking of innovative ideas or concepts. A workshop is a suitable way to move from insights to innovation. You will learn more on this in the next section about translating trends.

QUESTION

Can you think of a communication approach for a specific challenge?
Think of the challenge and define what will be the most suitable communication approach. Consider your client's company culture and their level of trend sensitivity. Then define the tone-of-voice you would like to use.

As for deliverables, which formats fit your client? Are combinations possible? Check if the available budget also matches the most suitable deliverables.

STEP 3: TRANSLATE

Can you help your client to think of innovative ways to tap into certain trends? After communicating the most relevant trends you make a next step into the translation of a trend. In the last decades the domain of trend research has been shifting more and more from detecting and analysing information to also helping others to apply it during innovation processes. This last step in the apply phase is a first step towards innovation where you go from thinking into doing and from analysis into development.

This step of the trend process is action oriented and aimed at creating meaningful futureproof innovations that add to people's quality of life. The translation step requires the combination of trend insights with imagination because you need creativity to shape the future. As mentioned before trend inspired innovation uses emerging values and needs in society as a base to innovate on. These trend values are a compass throughout an innovation process and serve as the foundation for concept development. The various examples of trends spots can give concrete inspiration on how to translate these values into products, services, events, campaigns and so on. But be aware that innovation is not about creating copies of these examples but about finding the sweet spot where emerging values and creative ideas collide.

> "The aim of Philips is not to create an exact copy of an already existing trend manifestation. The focus should therefore lie on the underlying needs of people and how to apply those to our business, for example people not wanting to own a car anymore, or people not wanting to work in traditional ways anymore."
> Claudia Lieshout - Creative Director Lifestyle Trends at Philips Design

VALUES MEET VALUE

So as not to get stuck in thinking in solutions right away, it is essential to keep a bird's eye view on the innovation process. Start at a high level of abstraction and define a direction in which to move forward first. You might have heard about processes like design thinking, concepting, imagineering and ideation. See the 'want to know more?' section at the end of this chapter for books and platforms diving into these processes. They all have in common that they start at this higher level of abstraction, to subsequently evolve into more tangible ideas with specific guidelines for products, services, marketing, communication, design and styling. Using trend insights as a knowledge base during your innovation process helps in keeping this level of abstraction in sight. During the translation step, trend values are integrated into a valuefit and concept statement, on which further decisions in the innovation process are based and reflected upon.

A valuefit (Sutmuller, 2014) is a combination of values as seen from different perspectives. The emerging values the trends represent are not isolated variables and have to fit or confront other aspects of the challenge, for instance the organisation's values, specific target group values, sector developments and so on. By looking into these areas and combining these with trend values perspectives arise on opportunities in the market. A valuefit provides a balanced starting point to create future proof concepts that improve people's quality of life: *where values meet value*. It enables you to create concepts that have a future perspective, but at the same time include ingredients for immediate change.

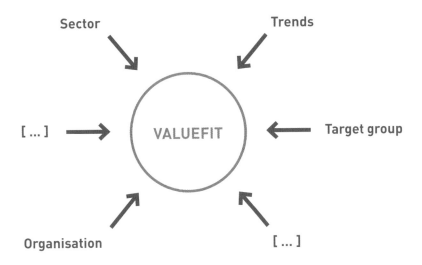

A valuefit overview.

There are so many trends, which should you select for a specific challenge and integrate into your valuefit? Trend inspired innovation is about selecting the most relevant trend(s) related to the challenge. You can use various tools to help you and your client decide which trends from the trend overview are most relevant. Choosing which trends to use depends on a variety of considerations.

For instance, you can take into account the way a trend interacts with a target group, how it fits the trend sensitivity of an organisation and how it matches actual developments in certain sectors and markets that are already innovating their products and services. Selecting trends evokes a discussion on the interactions between trends (Is there synergy?) and also about the desirability of a trend (Is it a threat or an opportunity?). After a final trend selection has been made, this selection becomes the main focus for the valuefit and is combined with the other values at play. You can use tools to help you to select trends together with your client.

To guide you through the process of translating trends and creating valuefits you can use existing canvases such as the Business Model Canvas by Strategyzer, the Valuefit Canvas by Serious Concepting or the Consumer Trend Canvas by TrendWatching. You can also create a tailor-made canvas adapted to your client's challenge inspired by existing canvases. These canvases allow you to use emerging values as a base combining it with other values for instance organisation values, specific target group values, sector developments or other values you should consider when responding to trends.

TOOLS: TREND SELECTION

Trend Stickering
An easy way to rank trends is to use stickering. Put up posters of the trends for your overview on a wall. Provide participants with a fixed amount of dotted stickers. Let everyone put one or more stickers on the trend(s) they feel are most relevant. This creates an instant visual over-view of the most 'popular' trends. Discuss with participants why they stickered a certain trend.

Trend Cards
Develop trend cards where you print each trend on a separate card with a visual and short description. Ask participants to select a fixed amount of cards from the pile and explain why they feel these are the most relevant trends.

Trend Grids
A more complex way of deciding which trends are most relevant is to combine them with another aspect that the client feels is important. For instance, you can create a timeline that shows words like Now, Next and Never and ask participants: which trends do you feel are relevant right now (Now), which are relevant in the future (Next) and which are not relevant at all for the project at hand (Never)?

The selected valuefit results in a concept statement (Sutmuller, 2014). This is a slogan-like statement accompanied by a short explanatory text that illustrates the choices made in the valuefit. The concept statement is an anchor for further innovation; all choices in terms of concept design and execution are connected to this statement. Information-wise it reveals the strategic path to take during the innovation process, by showing the direction for concept development. The statement marks the transition from the research phase to the design and development phase and embodies a combination of information and inspiration.

An example of a concept statement is the statement 'Run Unleashed' by Nike. It includes the following explanatory text: "Don't think about your form, or how your foot strikes the ground. Forget about technical jargon that makes running complicated. Just run. Feel your stride, the cushioning and stability. Allow yourself to Run Unleashed."

QUESTION

Can you make a valuefit for a specific challenge?

» What are the key values of trends you selected for this challenge? What other elements are crucial for the challenge? Can you add organisational values, target group values, sector values or other ones to the mix?

» Write these values down on a flip-over. Can you find matching values or opposing ones?

» Combine different values and experiment with various valuefits. Which ones spark the most excitement? Choose a final valuefit.

TRENDS & DUTCH GOVERNMENT

Rita Timmerman - Senior Research Consultant at the Dutch Ministry
of General Affairs

"My trend journey started with a paragraph on trends in the Information Council's yearly
report. I felt trends should get more focus and attention than just one paragraph. I wanted to
dive deeper and use more sources to really understand what is happening in society and how
this affects the way the government communicates with its citizens. The initial thought was
to go from a trend paragraph to a couple of pages of trend insights but in the end it became
an official stand-alone trend report on seven communication related trend clusters ranging
across a broad spectrum from citizens self-reliance and the government as a network player
to the new engagement of citizens and changing ways of communication.

But a report is not enough to really translate trend insights into our ministries and related
organisations. So I created a trend card game based on the findings of the trend report. This
game made the players more aware of what is relevant for themselves and what it means
for their daily work. We piloted this game and found the best way to use it as input for trend
application was to have all trends cards on a table and let every participant choose two to three
cards. They would then have to share why they chose this card and discuss the implications
together.

We shared the trend overview via the report and workshops across all ministries and related
organisations and published it via our website Rijksoverheid.nl. This project provided input on
various levels, also unexpected ones. It served as input for a list of trend topics for the annual
plans of government, which created a more long-term focus. It also stimulated the roll out of
new communication projects like 'information made to measure' which aligns with the trend
topic to curate the most relevant information for every citizen. Surprisingly, the trend insights
inspired our Academy of Government Communications to create an update of competencies
in job descriptions of government communication professionals and organise new training
sessions to get communication professionals futureproof. For instance sessions like how to
shoot film with your mobile phone.

Embarking on this trend project produced more awareness of societal trends. People really
appreciated getting an overview of the most relevant topics for the coming years and why they
matter right now. It gave them a sense of direction."

CREATIVE PROCESS

The concept statement forms the foundation to think of innovative ideas that represent the concept statement. For this to happen you need to step into a creative process. To dissect a creative process is almost a contradiction in terms because it is a very dynamic, iterative and non-linear process. The next pages will provide some building blocks on how to use your trend fuelled concept statement during this process.

"It's an iterative process in which one adds loads of creativity, business wisdom and gut feeling."

Jakob Sutmuller - Senior Lecturer Concepting & Business Innovation at Fontys ILS

TRANSLATION WORKSHOP

Workshops are often organised when a client not only wants to know about the latest trends but also wants to take a first step into translating and thinking of innovative ideas or concepts. Making a valuefit and coming up with a concept statement is integrated in these workshops and it ends with idea generation based on these. The setup of these workshops is flexible and depends on the type of client and their challenge. The workshop can have a duration ranging from a couple of hours, a full day to even multiple days. It often includes combinations of previously mentioned trend communication forms, like a trend presentation or a trend video. Participants are activated by various exercises to apply the trends to their challenge and create a valuefit by combining trend values with values of other aspects related to the challenge.

> *"We often finish our trend projects with a workshop where, after an inspiring trend presentation, we motivate people to work with these trends via various exercises to apply them to our business."*
>
> Claudia Lieshout - Creative Director Lifestyle Trends at Philips Design

A workshop should be guided by one or more professional moderators, who preferably have a neutral standpoint in the client's challenge. This type of setting is often most effective with a maximum of participants, say around fifteen, to keep an open dialogue and interaction flowing. Try to think beyond your client's organisational borders and look for ways of involving frontrunners, experts and innovators during the innovation process. Let them participate in a workshop and showcase their vision on the client's challenge. These types of people are often great in thinking outside the box and providing fresh perspectives on a challenge.

"In our innovation workshops we invite clients together with innovators and thought leaders and collectively try to design a solution for a current issue."

Franklin Ozekhome - Pop Culture Strategist at TINK

The creative process consists of a divergence and a convergence phase and these can be integrated in a workshop. You often start out with a trigger question to spark as many ideas as you can, which is called diverging. You can use various tools to activate participants to use the concept statement as a starting point for creative brainstorming. Then you finish by clustering and categorising every idea and select the ones you want to develop further, which is called converging. Take a look at some examples of tools to use during diverging and converging in brainstorms.

Trigger questions

To start your creative process and stimulate idea generation it helps to define various trigger questions. These type of questions often have an open formulation, like 'how can we.....' or 'what if....'? On the dots you can insert topics related to the concept statement and the client's case. For example: How can we diminish the growing amount of electronic litter? How can we connect people more in an offline way? Try out constructing various trigger questions to spark your imagination in different ways. These types of questions are important to ask yourself in an innovation process because they help to fuel your imagination.

"What if humans go to Mars? What would it mean for Asics? How would people exercise on that planet? How would you design products that tackle a different type of gravity?

Niels van der Burg - Global Category Insights Manager at Asics

Prioritise

When you are flooded with ideas you can use tools to organise and prioritise these ideas and start converging. Now it is time to be more critical about all ideas. The COCD-box (COCD, n.d.) is an example of a technique to categorise ideas by using a box with two axes: the originality of the idea versus its ease of implementation. Original but not (yet) feasible ideas are placed in the how? square, original and feasible are placed in the wow! square, the feasible and already known ideas should be placed in the now square. Ideally participants should be encouraged to think about unfeasible ideas connected to future possibilities, this allows new 'out of the box' ideas to blossom (Byttebier, 2002).

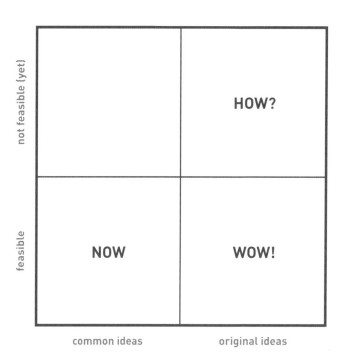

The COCD box.

When you have prioritised and categorised your ideas the next step is to move into developing these ideas. The scope of this book is not about turning you into a developer and designer of trend based concepts, because that is a discipline on its own. You can use the suggestions in the 'want to know more?' section to inform yourself about concept development. To give you some insight into what development can lead to, take a look at the emerging field of prototyping the future.

QUESTION ···

Which 'How can we' questions can you ask?

Write down questions using different elements from your valuefit and concept statement.

How can we ....?
How can we ....?
How can we ....?

Which 'What If' questions can you ask?

Write down questions about a selected trend related to the client's challenge. Then try to imagine what it would mean for the issue at hand in people's daily life five to ten years from now.

What if ....? Then ....
What if ....? Then ....
What if ....? Then ....

Brainstorm rules

Innovation happens when unexpected combinations are made. To generate ideas based on your trigger question(s) you can use various brainstorming techniques. But before you start jotting down ideas, check the essential rules of any brainstorm (IDEO, 2015).

TOOL: BRAINSTORM RULES

Defer judgement. You never know where a good idea is going to come from. The key is to make everyone feel like they can say the idea on their mind and allow others to build on it.

Encourage wild ideas. Wild ideas can often give rise to creative leaps. In thinking about ideas that are wacky or out there you tend to think about what you really want without the constraints of technology or materials.

Build on the ideas of others. Being positive and building on the ideas of others take some skill. In conversation, try to use "and" instead of "but".

Stay focused on the topic. Try to keep the discussion on target, otherwise you can diverge beyond the scope of what you are trying to innovate.

One conversation at a time. Your team is far more likely to build on an idea and make a creative leap if everyone is paying full attention to whoever is sharing a new idea.

Be visual. In live brainstorms write down ideas on post-its and then put them on a wall. Nothing gets an idea across faster than drawing it.

Go for quantity. Aim for as many new ideas as possible. In a good session up to 100 ideas are generated in 60 minutes. Crank the ideas out quickly and build on the best ones.

"You have to be really open minded to find the unexpected connections between the trends and the challenge. Innovation can start by combining two totally different things."

Loui Sampaio - Former exchange student at Fontys Minor Trend Watching

PROTOTYPING THE FUTURE

A very open and creative way of translating the future into tangible objects is prototyping the future or so-called speculative design. Design has evolved beyond aesthetics. Speculative design or design fiction aims to explore how the future might play out by translating new developments into objects or systems and placing these within everyday situations.

These then spark debate about their implications helping people to reflect on whether this would be a preferable future or an avoidable future. This way of working is really action oriented because you start building things right away. The prototypes can take all kinds of forms such as trend objects or rooms where people can get immersed in the future. For example, if you are working for a client in the food sector you can design an experience showing how people might cook in the future. You can create a future kitchen in your client's office space and have people interact with it. This lets them experience how it feels to be someone who lives in this future.

> *"Trends provide a direction and from this direction you should start doing things, put up a webpage and start experimenting, start out with rapid prototyping. Just do it!"*
> Tim Schuurman - Partner at DesignThinkers Group

An engaging way to bring the future to life in an organisation is by creating a role play situation. You can enact a day in the near or far future and play possible trend scenarios so you can observe what people would actually do in a specific future scenario. Participants are first provided with information about trends and then create a role, a future persona. All participants can then engage in a kind of theatrical play together. This really helps people to take responsible future oriented decisions because they experience being in a situation where they have to prepare for a specific future scenario. The more you can get people immersed in these future worlds, the more people will be activated to act on the trends.

> *"Future roleplaying makes the future become more personal, people's professional shells fall off while doing this, people can really open up and learning is accelerated."*
> Cornelia Daheim - Principal of Future Impact

These more immersive forms of imagining the future also help check how a target group is responding to a trend inspired innovation in an early stage. Are they accepting the first ideas and drafts? If you experiment and test trends with the mainstream you can find out which parts are still too forward thinking and which parts they already embrace. Introducing an innovation too soon or too late could mean missing out on your customer at the point when they are ready to embrace a trend.

> *"You need to know what people are ready to buy right now. Many brands aim for the mass market so the product should not be too farfetched."*
> Ksenia Penkina Lery - CEO of Trendsquire

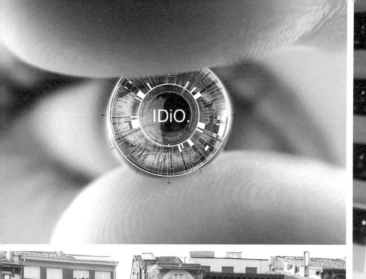

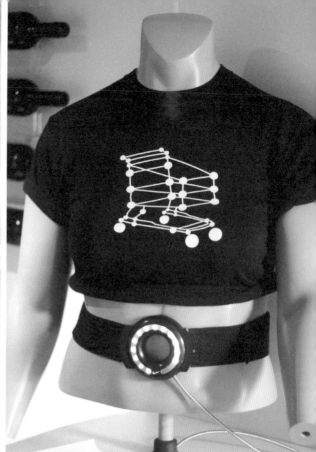

INTERVIEW | Koert van Mensvoort

Koert van Mensvoort
Founder and Creative Director of Next Nature Network

Why did you start Next Nature Network?

"Next Nature Network is an international network for anyone interested in joining the debate on a future in which nature and technology are fusing. When talking about future technologies, people often have misconceptions about what something is but still hold a strong opinion. They are not informed. I feel we can do so much better so I want to stimulate a better discussion about the future via our network."

How do you spark this debate?

"Imagination and art can help in making potential futures tangible so more people can participate in the conversation. There are multiple futures and we should make them visible to enable reflection on where we want to go. That's what we try to do with all our projects, for example, our NANO supermarket. The NANO Supermarket presents speculative nanotech products that may hit the shelves within the next ten years: medicinal candy, interactive wall paint, a wine which taste can be altered with microwaves, invisible security spray and much more. They function as scenarios for potential NANO futures that help us decide what technological future we actually want. We put it on a city square and people just randomly walk in. This is not just for the experts, it is open for everyone to join the discussion."

How would you describe your ways of working?

"When thinking about new topics for a project we start with an open, crazy brainstorm to envision what might happen in the future. Anyone can mention any topic they feel might be interesting. We map these ideas to create a sort of landscape which we call the 'design space'. This generates questions and we fill the blank spots by doing research. To find out more about technological feasibilities of our ideas we talk to engineers and execute an emerging technology assessment. Then we start out our design research and prototype the ideas. By making something people can really meet the future and give feedback so we can update the prototype. This way of researching allows you to reflect in a different way on your future concept than in your head or on paper."

Which criteria do you use for your designs?

"Creating future designs is never about provoking and shocking people, because people close down and your chance to interact or connect with them is lost. If you make your speculative designs really beautiful, detailed and respectful people will be more open to strange future forward things. As Raymond Loewy, the famous designer, said a design should be most advanced yet acceptable."

Are you also realising any of these prototypes?

"Yes, with our latest project Eco Coin, an alternative currency to express environmental value, we are in the midst of really implementing this currency in real-world systems. We are handing out eco medals for eco heroes, use eco coins at festivals, creating a bitcoin version of the eco coin and so on. It would be great if in the future people would say: how did the world ever not use an eco-coin?"

TRENDS & SOUNDCLOUD

Nadines Guhlich - Audience Research Lead at Soundcloud

"Trend insights always need to be translated into something, in my case to different markets, to Soundcloud users or to new product features. I must go beyond just delivering trend slides and translate these into what it would mean for our industry and base business questions on it like: do we need to change something in our product? You can translate trends into new product features, but there is no recipe for when a trend is ready to be translated into a product. The right momentum is something that involves all kinds of other factors besides just your brand. For the music streaming business it was very convenient when 3G mobile data plans made it affordable for teenagers to stream on the go all the time, but this was something we at Soundcloud did not control ourselves at that time.

My goal is to have my colleagues own the trend insights themselves. When they live and breathe the trends they can work with them and make the right decisions. I am always asking myself: who is my target audience within the company and what kind of decisions do they have to make? When teams within Soundcloud are making their product road maps or overall strategy plans, I have to be a part of the process and check if they understand the trends they are working with. That's why I like to have meetings and workshops with small groups so people feel more comfortable to ask questions. It's a balance between being accessible and having open conversations and on the other hand people valuing my expertise and future visions.

Bigger companies have the budget to experiment in innovation projects, think of the Google spin offs. Although they might not act on it immediately, it makes them better prepared for the future. When you're a smaller company, like Soundcloud, it's much more difficult to respond to these changes because it's more of a risk for us to innovate in an early stage."

THE FINISH LINE?

You have now arrived at the end of the three phased cycle of trend research and went from scanning and analysing to applying trends. Innovation is a fuzzy, dynamic, chaotic and iterative process. The earlier mentioned translation tools can help you in defining building blocks for your innovation process, but always try to stay flexible and adapt to the circumstances. It also means that there is not a hundred percent guarantee that using trends will lead you to a ground-breaking idea. This sometimes makes it hard to explain the added value of trends to others because trend insights are only one factor in the innovation process. In retrospect it is hard to pinpoint what the starting point of an innovation was, there is often not just one leading insight, there are always other factors playing out too.

"There is no good or bad concept, but rather a good or bad concepting process. A concept can fail for a lot of reasons, being consistent and iterative in the choices you make during a concepting process can help in avoiding failure."

Jakob Sutmuller - Senior Lecturer Concepting & Business Innovation at Fontys ILS

X SUMMARY

» The apply phase is about putting your trends to use to create value.

» In this phase trends are prepared to be integrated during an innovation process.

» Applying trends can be done in a structured three step way: scope, communicate, translate.

SCOPE

» Setting a scope helps you in understanding a client's challenge and perspective.

» To define a scope setting up an in-depth briefing is a must.

COMMUNICATE

» Based on the scope you communicate your trend insights in a tailor-made way.

» You choose a communication approach and the type of trend deliverables that fit your client's challenge.

TRANSLATE

» To translate trends into innovative ideas a valuefit and concept statement serve as a foundation.

» A translation workshop is a suitable way to move from insights to innovative ideas.

» By diverging and converging in the creative process you can select ideas to develop further.

X WANT TO KNOW MORE?

Eager to learn more about the apply phase of trend research?
Here you can find some suggestions for further reading, watching and clicking.
This is a selection of a vast array of sources. You can find more information at
www.howtoresearchtrends.com.

SOURCES ON COMMUNICATION ···

» The New York Times Manual of Style and Usage, a book by Allan Siegal and William Connolly
» Sway, an application to create presentations collaboratively

SOURCES ON INNOVATION ···

» The Innovation Expedition, a book by Gijs van Wulfen
» The Art of Innovation, a book by Tom Kelly
» The Future of Innovation, a book by Anna Trifilova
» Three Horizons, a book by Bill Sharp
» Innovation Design, a book by Elke den Oude
» Hidden in Plain Sight, a book by Jan Chipchase

SOURCES ON CREATIVE DEVELOPMENT ·······························

» Serious Concepting, a book by Jakob Sutmuller and Rudy van Belkom
» Seriousconcepting.com, a platform on concepting by Fontys International Lifestyle Studies
» Concept Code, a book by Gaby Crucq-Toffolo and Sanne Knitel
» The Field Guide to Human-Centered Design, a book by IDEO.org
» This is Service Design Thinking, a book by Marc Stickdorn and Jakob Schneider
» COCD, offers training and guidance in creative thinking
» Design Thinkers Academy, offers workshops and boot camps on the design thinking process
» IDEO U, offers online courses in design thinking and creative thinking

SOURCES ON USING CANVASES ·······································

» Serious Concepting, a book by Jakob Sutmuller and Rudy van Belkom
» Business Model Generation, a book by Alexander Osterwalder
» Value Proposition Design, a book by Alexander Osterwalder
» Trend-Driven Innovation, a book by Henry Mason, David Mattin, Maxwell Luthy and Delia Dumitrescu

SOURCES ON BRAINSTORMING ···

» Lateral thinking, a book by Edward de Bono
» Creativity in Business, a book by Ramon Vullings and Igor Byttebier
» Not invented here, a book by Ramon Vullings and Marc Heleven

SOURCES ON SPECULATIVE DESIGN ·····································

» Next Nature Network, a network for anyone interested to join the debate on a future in which nature and technology are fusing.
» Near Future Laboratory, a speculative design thinking practice
» Speculative Everything, a book by Anthony Dunne and Fiona Raby
» The World We Made, a book by Jonathan Porritt

#6

FOR
WARD

THE FUTURE UNFOLDS

What does the future of researching the future hold? This chapter looks forward and showcases visions of trend professionals on the development of their own profession. It concludes with these experts helping you move forward too by sharing their essential advice on how to research trends.

> TOPICS

> INTRO

As a researcher of the future you can apply your skills and insights to think about the future of the trend profession too. The trend domain also has to update itself continuously to stay relevant and progress. What do you think will be the future of trend research? Will it be data-driven and employ trend algorithms instead of researchers of flesh and blood? Will it be collaborative and more focused on working together with other disciplines? Or will it be...? In the first section of this chapter trend professionals share their future visions and give you some food for thought.

"Why would people hire a trend researcher in the future? This is a question we need to ask ourselves as trend professionals."

Tessa Cramer - Future-minded Academic and Senior Lecturer Trend Research at Fontys ILS

And what about your own trend skills? How can you move forward after reading this book and start integrating trend research into your daily activities? The same trend professionals will share their number one advice with you in the last section of this book. This way you will not make the same mistakes they did when they started out in trend research.

THE PROFESSION MOVING FORWARD

What does the future of researching the future hold? Trend research is a profession 'under construction' and ever changing. So why not ask experts on researching the future to think about the future of their own profession? All interviewees were asked the same question: what do you think the future of trend research will be? They found it a very interesting question and enthusiastically started talking about their future visions of the profession. All answers were analysed and the results show some clear categories of future visions and directions the profession might move into. The future of trend research might be... data-driven, integrated, engaging, unified, creative, culture sensitive, educated or adding more value. Curious about what this all means? On the next pages you can read about these possible futures of trend research. Each future direction is brought to life by selecting the most illustrative quotes by trend professionals on these matters.

DATA DRIVEN?

When you hear buzzwords like big data, self-learning algorithms and real-time analytics next to statistics about redundancies and professions getting extinct, you might wonder what the future will be for trendwatchers. Will computer calculations take over the trendwatchers' job as business managers demand numbers and statistics? Or is it too difficult to explain people's erratic behaviour with numbers? Trend experts seem to be divided on this matter. On the one hand they feel human-focused, qualitative research cannot be overtaken by machines, as the following quotes show.

> *"Trend research is a creative process and people are known to develop skills beyond what data can do."*
>
> Sam Shaw - Head of Insight at Canvas8

> *"With all the numbers in the world brands still find it difficult to engage with youngsters. You need cultural infused trend research to help you with these types of questions."*
>
> Hannah Lincoln - Culture Research Manager at China Youthology

> *"I don't believe that big data will change our profession a lot. Big data is based on statistical parameters that are based on the past. For example, the future of mobility can only be quantified by researching existing mobility concepts and not by researching non-existing concepts."*
>
> Patrick van der Duin - Executive Director at STT and Associate Professor Futures Research & Trend Watching at Fontys ACI

On the other hand some trend researchers see a data-driven future as an enrichment of their qualitative based trend stories. It might help to create more comprehensive trend storylines.

> *"Trend research will be more analytic because of the growth of technology and data. Our qualitative research insights will be amplified by real-time data."*
>
> Franklin Ozekhome - Pop Culture Strategist at TINK

Some of the experts are already experimenting with combining their trend insights with quantified information as the following two examples show.

TREND TRAJECTORIES
Kelly McKnight - Head of Culture & Trends at Join the Dots

"Our newest service is to quantify the trends. This way you can get a grip on which trends are growing and which are more established. It chimes with the need for more evidence in trend research. We ask people to score statements about the core of a trend, map their attitudes and combine these with the numbers about actual behaviour, showing who are already acting upon the trend. This way you can divide trends into emerging, niche, growing and more established ones and split these by different demographics, for example baby boomers and millennials.

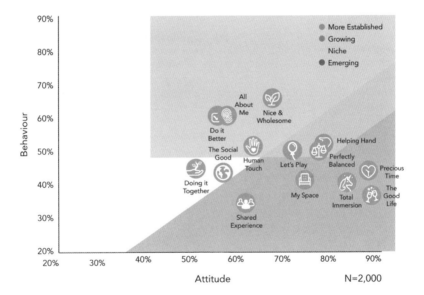

This graphic plots out the trends based on the percentage of those agreeing with the attitude and behaviour statements for each. So the more the trend attitude resonates with people the further to the right it sits, and the more people behaving in a way that aligns with the trend the closer to the top they sit. We're only just beginning to understand the practical application of this work and have been experimenting with clients to apply it as part of their annual planning cycle. We see a lot of potential in this way of researching trends."

HYBRID ANALYSIS

Ksenia Penkina Lery - CEO of Trendsquire

"We mainly focus on clients within the design, fashion and beauty domains. We are launching a new service to understand what the correlation is between the life strategies of consumers and their design preference. With quantitative analysis we try to find relations between trends mind-sets and design preferences. Our clients demanded this type of information so we started to work with a start-up in big data analysis. We are looking into correlations between our trends and the involvement of the general population in these trends. For instance, a person whose attitudes match a certain trend prefers specific types of designs and styles. Data helps getting more details on the shifts of trends but you still need qualitative research to define the trends you want to quantify."

INTEGRATION?

Many trend experts feel that trend research will become more integrated into companies' daily work processes instead of being a yearly add-on. Organisations are already hiring trend researchers more often as part of their insights or innovation teams. But integrating a future oriented approach into an organisation means moving beyond hiring a specific person to monitor trends. Trend experts think that company cultures should become more open to embracing change and more employees should become skilled in using trend research in their daily job routine.

"Being informed on trends should become ingrained in the DNA of an organisation. It pushes you to always have your radar on in your industry and other industries."

Pernille Kok-Jensen - Connectivity Director at MARE

"Many companies just hire a trend director or head of innovation and think the job is done, but it is important to develop an internal company culture that is open to change."

Kristina Dryža - Global Director of Trends and Futures at House of Brand Group

"Everyone will be more of a trendwatcher, from students to professionals. They will all be integrating trend research more in their daily work."

Victoria Foster - Head of tw:in at TrendWatching

"Every company should have a Chief Future Officer. You need people with a helicopter view who are open for change and innovation. They can build bridges to other disciplines like marketing or product development."

Djenny Brugmans and Nanon Soeters - Partners at Rozenbrood

INTERDISCIPLINARY?

Trend research is being increasingly combined with other disciplines, like marketing and design. Many trend pro's think that trend researchers in the future will be part of interdisciplinary teams more often throughout innovation processes. Experiencing 'a day in the life of' might be a start for a better understanding and cross-pollination between all types of disciplines. To create a way forward you need to really find the sweet spot where trend research and other disciplines come together.

> *"Create more interdisciplinary teams which combine different backgrounds to hack the problems of our time."*
>
> Tessa Cramer - Future-minded Academic and Senior Lecturer Trend Research at Fontys ILS

> *"Trend researchers should move closer to cultural studies and design studies. If we all join forces we can become a very strong movement with a unique transdisciplinary methodological approach."*
>
> Nelson Pinheiro - Assistant Professor of Trends Studies and Cultural Management at the University of Lisbon

> *"For a trend researcher it would be interesting to work in a business development environment to understand the context of making trend based ideas viable. For a concepter it would be interesting to work in a non-biased setting and trying to understand change without having your judgement clouded by business targets."*
>
> Jakob Sutmuller - Senior Lecturer Concepting & Business Innovation at Fontys ILS

> *"The future of trend research is in starting new collaborations and working according to the T-shaped model of going broad and deep at the same time."*
>
> Carl Rohde - Culture Sociologist and founder of Science of the Time

ENGAGING?

Many feel that presenting trends in a sender-receiver format is a thing of the past and text-heavy reporting has reached its saturation point. The future of trend research will bring more immersive and engaging ways of trend communication. The conference format of presenters on a stage and the audience sitting in rows also needs an upgrade and trend researchers can be frontrunners in turning this old-fashioned style of presenting around.

> *"Trends have to be embodied and lived. When you are talking about a trend called co-collaboration for a food industry audience, maybe it is better to make sushi rolls together while talking about this trend then to be on a stage with your PowerPoint deck."*
>
> Kristina Dryža - Global Director of Trends and Futures at House of Brand Group

> *"We will move to trend experiences and live events. Going through a trend activity during a workshop provides more feeling on how to tackle trends than just reading a report."*
>
> Victoria Foster - Head of tw:in at TrendWatching

"I feel I can still do more with visualising trends, like experiment more with making my own images or animations or working side by side with an illustrator."

Cécile Cremer - Founder of Trends & Innovation Agency Wandering the Future and former Fontys ILS student

UNIFIED PROFESSION?

Trend researchers do not have consensus yet on a shared language or research approach. While many feel that trend research should not be too rigid and stay flexible, they also think a more common ground helps to solidify the profession to the outside world. With so many people calling themselves trend-watchers they see a risk of inflation of the profession. Exchanging views on this matter more often with fellow trend professionals is something that many feel would help in finding a more unified voice.

"It's important that the whole trend industry comes together and unpack what trend research is to help clients appreciate the diverse ways of going about trend research."

Sam Shaw - Head of Insight at Canvas8

"I would like to see more exchange amongst trend practitioners themselves. If you are tolerant and open minded you can see that we are all working in more or less the same field."

Cornelia Daheim - Principal of Future Impact

"Maybe it is in the name? I feel that our process is more strategic and analytic than the name trendwatcher or trend spotter suggests."

Pernille Kok-Jensen - Connectivity Director at MARE

"Many academics look at the trend profession with reservations. We need to develop our field and work closely with trend agencies. If we don't work together as a discipline, trend studies will be seen as a novelty field with no added value."

Nelson Pinheiro - Assistant Professor of Trends Studies and Cultural Management at the University of Lisbon

CREATE CHANGE?

Researching the future is becoming more of an interactive two-way street and trend experts feel that creating impact has to be a more important objective of trend research. Applying trends will become a more crucial element in the trend research process. In the future the role of a trend researcher might be that of the change maker and people's activator. This way trend research will guide yourself or others towards not just understanding change but also towards acting on change or even being the change yourself.

"We will move towards empowering people in what they can do right now to make a change."

Laura Wolfs - Senior Research Consultant at Point Blank International

"I would like to get rid of the idea that researchers are only there to support and service the other teams within a company. I would like researchers to take more ownership of their expertise and really drive change."

Nadines Guhlich - Audience Research Lead at Soundcloud

"Inspired by trends you can have amazing ideas. I feel the next step is to put these ideas into a conceptual form. How to come up with a product iteration process and have in-person help to apply trends during this process."

Victoria Foster - Head of tw:in at TrendWatching

"Make trends more tangible by using experimentation earlier in the process of trend research, push from trend analysis towards thinking about what to do with these trends."

Tim Schuurman - Partner at DesignThinkers Group

CULTURAL SENSITIVITY?

Trend research has a global scope but some trend professionals feel it is often focused on mainly Western cultural trends. A future development might lie in making trend research more inclusive and get various cultural perspectives into play. Trend researchers think they should question themselves more often about how trends play out in different cultures. They should look beyond western cultures to define how global trends play out in local cultures.

"As an anthropocentric profession, we have to look at people's preferences and know what they will and will not accept. For example, in Russia femininity is still important so androgynous looks are not accepted so easily, although this might seem a global trend. "

Ksenia Penkina Lery - CEO of Trendsquire

"Global trends do not always take cultural differences into account. With a westernised view we tend to forget about the reality of other trends in other places of the world. What works in Germany does not have to work in Bolivia."

Valeria Ossio - Service & Strategic Designer at Mandalah

"I feel there is too much of a Western perspective to trend research. It almost seems like an echo chamber where everybody repeats the same thing over and over. I would like to see more diversity in the trend profession itself and the trends presented."

Kristina Dryža - Global Director of Trends and Futures at House of Brand Group

"The profession will evolve into understanding more about cultures and tribes and also looking into influential cultural networks more."

Franklin Ozekhome - Pop Culture Strategist at TINK

GET EDUCATED?

Many trend professionals are self-educated because there was no formal education on researching the future known to them or available. Many did not even know it was a profession in the first place and tumbled into it by chance. Nowadays there are educational programs, a variety of trend modules and online courses available. But in many countries, industries or organisations trend research is still not very known yet. Getting people educated in thinking about the future is something that can be further developed.

"Thinking about the future should be much more integrated within our educational systems from an early age on. It helps in making more conscious decisions about your own future and helps you realise that besides a yesterday and a today, there is also a tomorrow."

Carlijn Naber - Economic Psychologist and Senior Lecturer Trend Research at Fontys ILS

"Workshops introducing you to coolhunting do not yet make you a trend professional. To know how to really do it and add value you need a proper education."

Nelson Pinheiro - Assistant Professor of Trends Studies and Cultural Management at the University of Lisbon

"There has always been a tomorrow but we have never learned how to deal with it. It's difficult for people to think about 2060 because it's hard to let go of present day references. To achieve this futures thinking has to become part of everyone's education."

Claudia Lieshout - Creative Director Lifestyle Trends at Philips Design

"I wonder if Lithuania is ready yet to integrate trend research in a business context. People in my country should first hear about it more often in the media, at conferences and in schools to get more confident to integrate it step-by-step in their daily routine."

Magė Fledžinskaitė - Former exchange student at Fontys Minor Trend Watching

ADD VALUE?

Trend researchers are looking for more and other ways to add value to their client's challenges, whether it is a commercial or a societal issue. Different routes are imaginable to becoming more of a sparring partner and sounding board for clients. From explaining your research process better to applying trends more to a specific challenge. Trend experts think that they should understand their clients better and link trend insights more to their strategic issues.

> "The profession will move into more consultancy work, where your interpersonal position within a client's company is becoming more important."
> Zuzanna Skalska - Founding Partner of 360Inspiration

> "We should connect more with the knowledge level of or our clients and translate our findings in a way they know better what to do with it."
> Cornelia Daheim - Principal of Future Impact

> "We should provide more strategic trends research and become more relevant to clients. Less focus on the coolhunting part, more on a down-to-earth approach and solutions."
> Juan Pablo Zapata Barros - Freelance Trend Researcher

MOVING FORWARD YOURSELF

The contents of this book are aimed at giving you a guideline on how to research trends. Throughout this book, you have been brought up to date on the history, the framework and the three phases of trend research plus the future visions on the profession itself. Now it is your turn to decide what to do with this information. Give it some time to sink in and reflect on what you experienced while reading the book. How do you feel about your future related to trend research? Which elements of the trend process do you feel you can integrate easily into your daily job, study or any other activities to become more sensitive to change? Which aspects might not fit into your current way of working easily? Talk about it with colleagues, friends, family, fellow students or anyone else that can help you move forward and find your own way of researching trends.

The interviewed trend professionals will nudge you in the right direction by sharing their personal advice on what to reflect on and what to pay attention to when you are starting to execute (parts of) trend research yourself. All interviewees were asked the same question: what is your number one piece of advice for anyone wanting to learn how to research trends? Their answers were analysed and the results showed some clear categories of advice. Trend professionals recommend you to: be curious, be critical, find a signature style, experiment with trend communication, know the boundaries of your trend advice and to find a mentor. On the next pages you can read more about each of these suggestions illustrated by trend professionals' quotes. Learn from the best in class so you do not have to reinvent the wheel.

BE CURIOUS

The number one advice given by all interviewees is to really be and stay curious all the time. It is essential to use various sources to keep yourself up to date. You do not need to become an expert in every topic, but you should at least roughly know what is going on in the world. Trend professionals advise you to train yourself to know a little about everything and become a trend generalist. Just sitting behind your desk is not the way to go. According to trend professionals you need to get out there in the world and experience the changes first hand.

"Have a broad field of interests and read a lot. Always ask why, because the why question will lead you to the changes."

Claudia Lieshout - Creative Director Lifestyle Trends at Philips Design

"Be open and scan wide, because what might not seem relevant right now, can become relevant tomorrow."

Heather Vescent - Futurist and founder of The Purple Tornado

"Travel to unknown places to get out of your comfort zone. Collect experiences by reading, watching, talking and working."

Djenny Brugmans and Nanon Soeters - Partners at Rozenbrood

"Don't just sit at a desk when doing trend research. You make too many assumptions when only reading stuff from the internet. You have to get first hand experiences by going out on the streets too."

Juan Pablo Zapata Barros - Freelance Trend Researcher

BE CRITICAL

Trend professionals also advise you to stay critical of your own research process and about all the information you find along the way. What you observed might seem the truth of today, but this may not be so tomorrow. Think about all assumptions people made throughout history that changed over time, like the earth being flat. Try to be aware of your own assumptions and perspectives throughout the research process because these can influence your trend analysis.

"Don't take anything for granted, stay critical, never stop researching."

Erica Bol - Change Maker at Teach the Future

"You sometimes get carried away in your own research, go into your bubble and think your analysis is fantastic. We should remind ourselves what and who we are doing it for, are we meeting the end objective?"

Cornelia Daheim - Principal of Future Impact

"When starting out in trend research I often didn't research trend manifestations thoroughly enough and made too many personal assumptions. So my advice is to really try to postpone your judgments and dig deeper."

Fleur Stiels - Concept Developer at Dutch Rose Media and former Fontys ILS student

"Take care in interpreting everything you see in a solid way. Trend research is more than just keeping your eyes open, you have to really understand what you are seeing."
Carl Rohde - Culture Sociologist and founder of Science of the Time

"Don't get carried away by future prognoses of others, some might be too optimistic or too pessimistic. Use them as hypotheses rather than the truth."
Patrick van der Duin - Executive Director at STT and Associate Professor Futures Research & Trend Watching at Fontys ACI

FIND A SIGNATURE STYLE

If you decide to integrate trend research into your daily activities trend experts say it is essential to think about your style of researching. What will be your niche, your story, your 'brand' as a researcher? Will you be a more visual driven researcher or more textual? Will you focus on a specific topic or be a more generic researcher? Explore which theme or metaphor fits your profile as a trend researcher and find your niche. Profile yourself accordingly via your trend deliverables and communication. Have your presentations, reports and blogs show your signature style in a consistent way.

"Have your own trend philosophy and find your specialism within the trend domain. Try to understand what your passion is skill-wise in trend research. Which types and techniques do you excel in and like?"
Sam Shaw - Head of Insight at Canvas8

"Dare to show your personality in your research process."
Fleur Stiels - Concept Developer at Dutch Rose Media and former Fontys ILS student

"Use your own field of expertise and integrate trend research tools into your practices. Use trend research skills to be a better designer, a better marketer, a better policy maker or a better advertiser."
Nelson Pinheiro - Assistant Professor of Trends Studies and Cultural Management at the University of Lisbon

"Find your trend DNA. Everyone has their specific skill set and you are allowed to find your own path and shape it the way you want."

Tessa Cramer - Future-minded Academic and Senior Lecturer Trend Research at Fontys ILS

EXPERIMENT WITH TREND COMMUNICATION

Trend professionals stress that experimenting with ways of communicating your trends is key in learning how to get your message across effectively. Many started out by making mistakes in their reports or live presentations and learned a lot from this. The objective for most presentations and reports is to have your audience accept and understand the trends, not to push them away by using irrelevant examples of trend spots or the wrong tone-of-voice.

> *"Trends have to blossom, we see a change but many can't relate to it yet. When you are in this field you are going to meet rejection and resistance. Be the bridge and don't isolate yourself with your work."*
>
> Kristina Dryža - Global Director of Trends and Futures at House of Brand Group

> *"In my first presentations I was too abstract and used fancy trend talk. My clients were looking at me like: 'what?' They didn't want to know about a freaky innovation in China but what was happening in their local Mexican market. So now I use a closer to home approach."*
>
> Juan Pablo Zapata Barros - Freelance Trend Researcher

> *"A huge learning point for me was to remember that I'm not presenting to other trendwatchers but to another species, the client. This meant keeping it more down to earth and repeating trends and manifestations that you have been talking about for several years."*
>
> Pernille Kok-Jensen - Connectivity Director at MARE

KNOW THE BOUNDARIES

When working for a specific client or working at a specific organisation it can be quite hard for beginners to understand the constraints and boundaries of a trend project. Trend professionals advise you to be open and enthusiastic but also practical and try to understand the level of flexibility you are granted. Not everything is possible when working at a brand or for a client and exploring how far you can stretch your research is an important aspect of trend research.

> *"Young researchers or interns sometimes like to overshare their first trend findings. That's cool in casual conversations but if you present such tendencies in a trend framework it has consequences and responsibilities we own as well, such as legal boundaries. They would propose an innovation that is about connecting all our user data without thinking a step further in constraints like data protection laws."*
>
> Nadines Guhlich - Audience Research Lead at Soundcloud

> *"If you are working with trends as an information base for future concepts you should be aware that most businesses are not looking more than a year ahead when it comes to their innovation efforts. Understand that looking too far ahead into the future can be hard to cope with for such companies."*
>
> Jakob Sutmuller - Senior Lecturer Concepting & Business Innovation at Fontys ILS

FIND A MENTOR

Some professionals found it very helpful to have an experienced person guide them along their trend journey. These can be professional trend researchers focused on the quality of your research skills. They can push you forward in executing field or desk research and strengthen your trend analysis. But some trend experts also suggest looking for a business coach who focuses more on developing your sales and project management skills.

"When you want to become really skilled in trend research, try to learn from a professional. Stay humble and don't get in the way of experienced researchers."

Cécile Cremer - Founder of Trends & Innovation Agency Wandering the Future and former Fontys ILS student

"Many young people want to start a business right away after they get their degree in Trends Studies. I would advise everyone to work at an agency first before starting a business in trend research. Gain knowledge and experience within the field, get to know people. When you feel you have the necessary elements, then start a business."

Nelson Pinheiro - Assistant Professor of Trends Studies and Cultural Management at the University of Lisbon

"Starting my own trend business without experience in sales and finance turned out to be the most expensive MBA I could find. I overestimated my commercial skills and if I could start over again I certainly would have prepared better and studied more on how to run a business."

Rodrigo dos Reis - Consumer Trends Specialist at Zeitgeist

> SUMMARY

» Trend research is a field that is still under construction and its future can be moulded.

» You can use trend research skills to think about the future of the profession of trend research.

» The future of trend research might be data-driven, integrated, engaging, unified, creative, culture sensitive, educated or adding more value.

» When starting out in trend research reflect on your own thoughts and feelings about the profession and research process.

» Trend professionals advise you to be curious, be critical, find a signature style, experiment with trend communication, know the boundaries of your trend advice and to find a mentor.

OUTRO

You have finished reading this book. I hope you are inspired about the profession of trend research and feel equipped to integrate it into your own specific skill set and daily activities. For me, personally, it was very inspiring to embark on this project and to talk to the trend professionals and (former) trend students mentioned in this book. Exchanging views with others helps me reflect on my own assumptions, opinions and thoughts. I have learned a lot while writing this book and as a researcher that is always the ultimate goal in life.

This book is meant as a guide on the basics of trend research. As mentioned often throughout the chapters, reading this book is just the beginning. To become skilled in detecting, understanding and acting on change you need to practice and learn by doing. And please, have lots of fun while experimenting with the various trend research activities and tools. I know I did and I cannot imagine a job that fits my insatiable curiosity better. I hope it will activate your sense of curiosity too.

If you have any thoughts on the contents of this book, please share your suggestions, additions and questions via howtoresearchtrends.com and via social media using #htrtbook. If you ever need assistance in how to start your own trend research project or have any questions about my personal experience as a trend researcher, do not hesitate to drop me a line either via els@howtoresearchtrends.com.

Let's create the future together!

ACKNOW LEDGEMENTS

A big shout-out to everyone who collaborated on this book, I could not have done it without you. Thanks to:

Fontys Academy for Creative Industries for providing guidance, time and support so I could embark on this journey. Especially Patrick van der Duin, lector of the Fontys research circle Futures Research and Trend Watching who was always there to encourage me with a helpful comment or witty remark.

BIS Publishers for being very enthusiastic from the start about publishing this niche book about trends.

My fellow trend lecturers at Fontys International Lifestyle Studies. Especially Carlijn Naber and Tessa Cramer whose brains I was allowed to pick at any time and who provided me with much needed reflection and constructive feedback. And also Iris van der Zanden, Iris van Bossum and Lotte van Oosterhout for giving a much needed outsider's perspective.

All students at Fontys International Lifestyle Studies and students of other programs I have lectured at for your always surprising questions and remarks during lectures and workshops. You taught me to explain how to research trends to others in an accessible way.

All the interviewed trend experts for providing a sneak peek into their work processes. Thanks so much for taking the time to answer my questions and sharing your thoughts with me.

Esther Scheide for taking on the graphic design for this book and making it look bold and beautiful at the same time. My style squad who gave their fresh perspective on the book design. Thank you **Maud van de Wiel, Tessa Petrusa, Saar van der Spek and Jeroen Timmer.**

All the agencies and clients I have worked for in the last decades, especially research agency MARE for giving me a platform to not only talk about 'the' trends but also about how to research trends.

Esther van der Wal for introducing me to trend research. Although I was quite hesitant about entering the trend domain at the time, thanks for persuading me.

My parents Roel and José Dragt, my brother Jelle Dragt and my friends, who were always there to provide kind and motivating words and put things in perspective when I really needed it.

My elementary school teacher, Teun Govers, who made me promise to write a book someday.

Protectio-
nism
Climate
Change
Adaptation
Housing
for
Everybody
Legalization
of Drugs
FOREVER
YOUNG
Open
Source
Movement
Circular
Economy
New and
Affordable
Advanced
Materials

SOURCES

REFERENCES

Asselt, M. van, Faas, A., Molen, F. van der. (2010). Uit zicht, toekomstverkennen met beleid (Out of sight: looking to the future carefully). Amsterdam: Amsterdam University Press.

Bell, W. (2003). Foundations of Futures Studies. Transaction Publishers.

Bell, W. (2002). A community of futurists and the state of the futures field. *Futures*, 34, 235-247.

Bishop, P., Hines, A. (2012). Teaching about the Future. Palgrave Macmillian.

Byttebier, I. (2002). Creativiteit Hoe?Zo!. Lannoo

Canvas8. (n.d.). Macro Behaviours. Retrieved from http://www.canvas8.com/macro-behaviour.html

COCD. (n.d.) De COCD box. Retrieved from http://www.cocd.org/kennisplatform/cocd-box/

Dawkins, R. (1976). The Selfish Gene. Oxford University Press

Delaney, B. (2016). Smell expert Sissel Tolaas breathes deep and then follows her nose in Melbourne. The Guardian.

Dimutrescu, D. (2012). Road Trip to Innovation. TrendONE.

Felce, D., Perry, J. (1995). Quality of Life: its Definition and Measurement. Elsevier Science Ltd.

Fletcher, A. (2001). The Art of Looking Sideways. Phaidon Press.

Fontys International Lifestyle Studies. (2016). Trendbook 2016. Retrieved from https://ddwtrendtours.files.wordpress.com/2016/10/trendbook-ddw-final-spreads.pdf

Fontys International Lifestyle Studies. (2017). Ambiente Trendbook 2017. Retrieved from http://www.ambientetrends.com/uploads/2/5/6/1/25612072/trendbook_ambiente_2017.pdf

Fontys International Lifestyle Studies. (2016). Ambiente Trendbook 2016. Retrieved from http://www.ambientetrends.com/ambiente-2016.html

Francis, A. (1967). Scanning the Business Environment. Macmillan.

Gladwell, M. (2002). The Tipping Point: How Little Things Can Make a Big Difference. Back Bay Books.

Hines, A. (2011). Consumer Shift. No Limit Publishing Group.

IDEO (2015). The Field Guide to Human-Centered Design. IDEO.org

Mason, H., Mattin, D., Luthy, M., Dumitrescu, D. (2015). Trend-Driven Innovation. John Wiley & Sons.

McLuhan, M., Fiore, Q. (1967). The Medium is the Massage. Random House.

Osterwalder, A. (2010). Business Model Generation. John Wiley.

Oxford Dictionary. Definitions of ´change´ and ´trend´. Retrieved from oxforddictionaries.com in September 2016.

Popcorn, F. (1992). The Popcorn Report, Faith Popcorn on the Future of Your Company, Your World, Your Life. Collins.

Rogers, M.E. (2003). Diffusion of Innovations. Free Press.

Rokeach, M. (1973). The Nature of Human Values. Free Press.

197

Roothart, H. and Pol, W. van der, (2002). Van Trends naar Brands. Kluwer.

Sutmuller, J., Belkom, R. van. (2014). Serious Concepting. Fontys Academy for Creative Industries.

Son, H. (2015). The History of Western Futures Studies: An exploration of the intellectual traditions and three-phase periodization. *Futures, 66,* 120-137.

Thomas, W.I. (1928), The Child in America: behavior problems and programs. A. A. Knopf.

TrendWatching. (n.d.). 5 Consumer Trends for 2017. Retrieved from http://trendwatching.com/trends/5-trends-for-2017/

TrendWatching. (September, 2016). Trends Go Social. Retrieved from http://trendwatching.com/blog/trends-go-social-part-one/

TrendWatching. (April, 2012). Flawsome. Retrieved from http://trendwatching.com/trends/flawsome/

Vullings, R., Heleven, M. (2015). Not Invented Here. BIS Publishers

Wack, P. (1985), Scenarios: Uncharted waters ahead, Harvard Business Review.

Wells, H.G. (1913), The Discovery of the Future. B. W. Huebsch.

WHO. (1997). Program on Mental Health. Retrieved from http://www.who.int/mental_health/media/68.pdf

INTERVIEWS

Bol, E. (2016, November 1).
Personal interview.

Brugmans, D. and Soeters, N. (2016, November 10).
Personal interview.

Burg, N. van der. (2016, December 15).
Personal interview.

Cramer, T. (2016, November 1).
Personal interview.

Cremer, C. (2016, October 18).
Personal interview.

Daheim, C. (2016, December 22).
Skype interview.

Dryža, K. (2017, January 5).
Skype interview.

Duin, P. van der. (2015, August 25).
Personal interview.

Fledžinskaitė, M. (2015, October 29).
Personal interview.

Foster, V. (2017, January 19).
Personal interview.

Guhlich, N. (2016, December 22).
Skype interview.

Kok-Jensen, P. (2017, January 18).
Personal interview.

Lieshout, C. (2016, November 3).
Personal interview.

Lincoln, H. (2016, December 8).
Skype interview.

McKnight, K. (2016, November 25).
Skype interview.

Mensvoort, van, K. (2016, December 15).
Personal interview.

Naber, C. (2016, October 18).
Personal interview.

Ossio, V. (2016, November 16).
Personal interview.

Ozekhome, F. (2016, December 8).
Skype interview.

Penkina Lery, K. (2016, December 2).
Skype interview.

Pinheiro, N. (2016, September 11).
Skype interview.

Reis, R. dos. (2016, August 29).
Personal interview.

Rohde, C. (2016, November 3).
Personal interview.

Sampaio, L. (2016, December 20).
Personal interview.

Schuurman, T. (2016, December 16).
Personal interview.

Shaw, S. (2016, November 29).
Skype interview.

Skalska, Z. (2016, December 6).
Skype interview.

Stiels, F. (2015, December 17).
Personal interview.

Sutmuller, J. (2017, January 17).
Personal interview.

Theis, B. (2016, December 16).
Skype interview.

Timmerman, R. (2016, January 18).
Personal interview.

Vescent, H. (2017, February 22).
Skype interview.

Wolfs, L. (2016, November 16).
Personal interview.

Zapata Barros, J. (2016, September 8).
Personal interview.

IMAGES

Page 15: Next Nature Network

Page 19: Evonik by ter Burg

Page 22: Fontys Academy for Creative Industries

Page 27: Patrick van der Duin

Page 29: Fontys Academy for Creative Industries

Page 40: Cecile Cremer

Page 44: Design Thinkers Group

Page 52: Mantas Lesauskas

Page 54: The trend research cycle is inspired by a visual of Elke Naber

Page 57: Fontys Academy for Creative Industries

Page 69: Eddy Wenting

Page 73, clockwise starting at the top on the left: Els Dragt, Els Dragt, MARE, MARE, MARE

Page 79, clockwise starting at the top on the left: Rodrigo dos Reis, MARE, Ksenia Penkina-Lery, Laura Wolfs

Page 87: TrendWatching

Page 91: Els Dragt

Page 94: 360Inspiration

Page 109: Design Thinkers Group

Page 112, clockwise starting at the top on the left: Mantas Lesauskas, Claudia Lieshout, MARE, Maud van de Wiel, Mantas Lesauskas, Fontys Academy for Creative Industries,

Page 115: Design Thinkers Group

Page 121, clockwise starting at the top on the left: Fontys Academy for Creative Industries, Mantas Lesauskas, 360Inspiration, Mantas Lesauskas, Fleur Stiels

Page 126: 360Inspiration

Page 130: Rozenbrood

Page 131: TrendWatching

Page 144: Els Dragt

Page 151, clockwise starting at the top on the left: Fontys Academy for Creative Industries, Ksenia Penkina-Lery, Loui Sampaio, MARE, Fontys Academy for Creative Industries, Rozenbrood

Page 155: Evonik by ter Burg

Page 158: Evonik by ter Burg

Page 163: Evonik by ter Burg

Page 168: all images by Next Nature Network

Page 169: Jeroen Broekmans

Page 179: Join The Dots

Page 183: Fontys Academy for Creative Industries

Page 185: 360Inspiration

Page 190: Evonik

Page 192: Fontys Academy for Creative Industries

Page 194: Mantas Lesauskas

Page 196: Evonik by ter Burg